SEASON 1

Day to Day

"THE BLURRY YEARS"

REAL LIFE STORIES
FROM INUVIK, NWT

SEASON 1

Day to Day

"THE BLURRY YEARS"

REAL LIFE STORIES FROM INUVIK, NWT

Randy "Zip" Day

BIG MOOSE
PUBLISHING

ISBN: 978-1-989840-68-9 (sc)
ISBN: 978-1-989840-69-6 (e)
Big Moose Publishing 03/24

DEDICATION

For Scotty Day. I am writing this book so some of my more memorable stories from Inuvik will always be with you, and hopefully one day, your kids as well.
Your dad loves you.

For Lois Day. Thank you for saying "Yes" all those years ago. I appreciate all the hours of help with the editing process of this book.
I love you.

From left to right: Randy "Zip" Day, Scotty Day, and Lois Day

Left: Randy with his son, Scotty, for whom the stories in this book were written.

Below: Scotty (left) with his dad, Randy, who wrote (and lived) these stories.

CONTENTS

A NOTE FROM THE AUTHOR

All stories are based from my memory. They occurred in the 1970s and 80s, and are told in no specific order.

Some names have been changed to protect innocent... and the guilty.

I did the best I could. Enjoy.

-Randy "Zip" Day

"KEEP SMILING."

"JUST BE KIND."

Above: Breakdown Beach, a meeting point on the way to my Uncle Dick's cabin at Ya Ya Lake.

Below: Reindeer Station, located not quite mid-way between Inuvik and Ya Ya Lake.

SCOTTY HAS HIS OWN PLAN

Our son Scott was originally going to be born in Edmonton; that was the plan according to the doctors and Lois' dietician in Inuvik. In fact, we were not even supposed to be pregnant. Lois was on the pill and suffering with Crohn's disease. Both those things together gave her little chance of even becoming pregnant, let alone try and keep a baby growing.

During the pregnancy, she couldn't keep food down. Not even water was staying long in her stomach. Lois was losing weight instead of gaining. All this meant that the baby was not getting the food and nutrients that was needed to grow.

Our hospital in town was not equipped to handle much if something was to go horribly wrong. The doctors didn't like our chances of even having the baby; all kinds of things were against us. I also must mention that we were in the planning stages for our upcoming wedding which added to the stress.

Lois was getting all the care that Inuvik hospital was able to help with. They did all they could with the resources they had at the time, being so far north.

The first three months were critical, and Lois had several trips to the hospital just so that they could check for any unforeseen problems that may be occurring. At this point, all they could tell us was the baby was growing, just not very fast. This was good and bad news all at the same time. The growing part was good, but the "not so fast" was a big concern.

Lois also never missed a trip up the Mackenzie River to Uncle Dickie's cabin the entire time she was pregnant. She just rode in the comfort of the big green boat with Uncle, while me (plus a few buddies) followed right behind in our much smaller and rough riding 18 foot open bow Lund boat.

I must jump backwards here for a moment. We had planned our wedding for July 11th and Lois' due date was supposed to be September 17th. She was supposed to fly out to Edmonton on the 13th to get prepped for the arrival of our son, Scotty. This remained the plan.

Once we had passed the three-month period and everything was going along as best as we could hope, we all could breathe a sigh of relief. Lois still felt like crap though. Crossing the three-month period meant we had a better chance of Lois carrying our baby all the way to September for the birth.

The next couple of months we just went about our business, trying to keep Lois healthy and get this wedding planned.

Everything was going well as we were getting closer to the due date. We had clothes bags packed for the plane trip to Edmonton well ahead of time. We managed to get our wedding behind us with just a few glitches. Maybe more than a few now

2

that I think about it. We had made it past July; Lois was doing okay. All we needed was to get into September and have a baby.

August was the month we would slowly start stockpiling any items we needed back in Inuvik for the winter months. We managed that without missing a beat of the fun that we always had at the lake. Uncle was a fair man. He always let us have all the fun we wanted at his cabin. Hell, sometimes he started the fun! When Uncle had chores that he wanted done around the cabin, no matter what he needed…we all helped!

The hardest part of having a cabin at Ya Ya lakes, was either the 90-mile boat ride up, or the 90-mile boat ride back to town. Some trips the water was like a mirror, which made for easy boating. Other times, the river was mad, as the wind would cause high waves and whitecaps, which could cause all sorts of trouble for us. Some of those troubles are within this book, while others will be in Season 2 of these short stories. (Yes, there is more to come.)

We were quickly running out of time to transport items back from the lake, as August was going by fast. Lois was still doing fine, but the river trips were getting harder to do, as this time of year the wind can really pick up. I promise you, that you do not want to be anywhere near that water if the wind comes howling from just the right direction. It takes a keen eye, a great reader of the water, and a bottle of rye to be able to navigate the river in adverse conditions.

Wednesday, August 26th at about 2am, Lois jumps out of bed, starts telling me her water had broke, and to go start the truck. Well, like a good husband, I went to go start the truck. As I was getting ready to do just that, I remembered that we had lent our truck to our roommate Brian P. His was in the garage getting some work done.

We are starting to go into panic mode here. What happened to the plan? Here we are running in circles, as this was a huge surprise. This was not supposed to be happening. The hospital was way across town, and we couldn't just walk, not now anyway!

Lois had a bit of a plan. She said, "Call the cab company and get Hippie over here." Hippie was the best cabbie ever, a very nice man, and drove one of the finest cars in town.

I called for Hippie, and he was at our door in record time knowing full well why we had called him. He got us both to the hospital quickly, and he even threw in a free cab ride for us! Awesome man, that Hippie.

We are in the Inuvik hospital three weeks before we had a chance to get to "The Plan". Lois was starting to have contractions and it was starting to look like an early delivery date for Scotty. By now, the real and better plan was abolished, and we were going to have a baby in August in Inuvik. I stayed at the hospital as long as possible until they had Lois resting comfortably for the rest of the night.

I went back to the hospital the next afternoon, August 26th, to check on Lois and our unborn Baby Scotty. Aunt Lucille had spent the day with her while I caught up at work to take some days off when Scotty got home. By now, another machine that monitors the baby's heartbeat and such had come available, and Lois was all hooked up to it. (I did say we had limited resources this far north.) I stood right beside that machine while I was keeping Lois company. All in all she was doing okay for not having any sleep. But while I was visiting, I started noticing something about the way that machine was working.

Now, I'm no doctor by any stretch, or a book writer either. I noticed that every time Lois had a big contraction, that machine would just go flat-lined. When the contraction was over the machine went back to a steady rhythm of a heartbeat. There was a nurse in the room, and I asked her about this machine and what was happening. She couldn't really answer me in a way that made me feel better, but she did say the doctor would be in later to check on what was causing this trouble.

This is where things get a bit crazy.

After watching Lois in pain with contractions and the heartbeat stopping at the same time, the only people that seemed worried was Lois and me. At this point, I had had enough of watching this. I told the nurse to call that doctor and get him here NOW! She had an excuse as to why she couldn't do that. I informed her that she had no choice right now. "Just get him here!"

After what seemed like a very long time, the doctor showed up with not a worry on his face. I explained what I had been watching for the last while and something seemed wrong with that machine, as every time there was a contraction little Scotty's heart was stopping.

The doctor watched the machine and when Lois had another contraction, there it was – a flat line on the heart machine. I stared straight into his eyes as I said, "There. Now look at that. What's going on that the baby looks to be suffering?" He kind of waved it off as if the machine wasn't working right, and there really wasn't any problem that he was worried about.

This is where it gets even crazier.

I literally ran straight at that doctor, grabbed him with both hands, picked him up ran out of the room, across the hall. I pinned him against the wall with his little legs dangling a foot off the ground. His eyes were big for a change. I kept him right there while I yelled, using all kinds of swear words, and in the

5

background, I could hear the nursing station calling for security to get here right away. That part didn't worry me. I was angry at this point, and it showed.

When security showed up, it was my own cousin coming up the hallway. When he saw it was me, he stopped just outside my kicking range, which was a smart move on his part. "Awww Randy, put the doctor down…please!" That fell on deaf ears as I was not letting this doctor away from that wall until he came up with a "new plan" for Lois and our baby.

We were at a sort of standstill. I wouldn't let the doctor go, and my cousin was not going to try and stop me. He knew me well enough than to do that. All in all, it was a pretty scary situation for everyone. With the doctor's word that he would have a closer look at what was going on in the room where Lois was, I slowly released my grip and lowered him back to the floor.

From the discomfort of her bed, Lois could hear all of what had happened in the hallway.

True to his words, the doctor remained in the room as Lois was having contractions, and yeah, he saw it on the machine... no heartbeat. They started the process of getting Lois ready for a C-section as this baby was not going to be born alive the natural way. At this point, Lois told my cousin (the security guard) to take me to the Legion and get a few drinks in me to calm my ass down.

We went with the "new plan" and our little Scotty came into the world via a C-section, in the evening of August 26th weighing in at 4lbs 8oz. It turns out that the umbilical cord was wrapped around his little neck, so every time Lois had a contraction, the cord would tighten on his neck choking the air out of him and stopping his tiny heart.

6

It's scary to think that I had to literally put a doctor up against the wall, in a way that he knew I was not going to let him go without some action happening. I wanted my son to born healthy and my wife to be safe while doing so. That's all that mattered.

The only funny part to this whole story is the fact that our son only missed being at our wedding by a little over a month…. now that's cutting things close!

Scotty, when you read this…just know that both your mom and dad would move mountains for you. You're a grown-up man now, and waiting to have your own children. While I don't think you need to fight a doctor, but if it's needed, do whatever it takes to keep your family safe. I did!

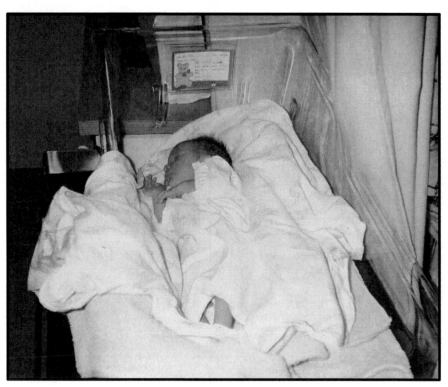

Baby Scotty Day

SCRUFF LEADS WITH HIS FACE

Spring finally arrived in Inuvik after a very long cold, harsh winter. Spring is a fun time when you live this far north. People start coming out more. The air is fresh, but warm, and no longer hurts the lungs to breathe the cold winter air.

With spring here, the snow melts quickly. The sun is up throughout the day as well as into the night.

This day was a Sunday. Our friend, Scruff, worked at the airport and lived in the supplied duplex housing units. Sitting on his deck, you could see a very long way. He lived in the last row of housing on the entire street and across the road there were no neighbours staring at your every movement. It was also quite relaxing as there wasn't much traffic on this end of town.

Some employees living in these housing units had families

with young kids. It was a safe place for the kids to play in the yards. Us adults could day drink and make noise and not bother anyone, but…

Like I mentioned the spring brings people outside that otherwise you may not see. Today, we were going to see one of those guys…Kurt was his name. He was about 17 years old or so. He owned the loudest and most decked out truck in town. He was proud of his truck and liked to drive it "like he stole it."

When sitting on Scruff's deck you could hear Kurt's truck start up. He loved revving that motor up loud for everybody to hear. He always, and I mean always, came past the duplexes as fast and noisy as possible…typical of a young man with a nice truck.

While sitting and enjoying a few drinks in the sunshine, and the warmth of the day on Scruff's deck, we heard the unmistakable sound of Kurt's truck. We knew he was headed our way and fast. I think he did this just to piss off Scruff. I don't know why, as Scruff was a big man; strong, tough, and when provoked, he looked way too big to piss off. Scruff hated that truck and the guy inside it. With kids living on this street, he was scared that one day the worst would happen. Couldn't blame him for that at all.

We could see the truck coming down the street towards us, fast of course. Scruff ran down his stairs and out into the middle of the street with arms held high. He was screaming as loud as possible for Kurt to stop. That truck stopped about two feet in front of him in the middle of the street.

We all waited up on the deck watching this unfold in front of us. Scruff went immediately to the driver's window and proceeded to yell at Kurt through the window. Kurt just sat there staring at him. Scruff was yelling about the speed factor, the kids, the noise and just plain going off on him, while Kurt

9

just sat inside his truck with his window rolled up.

Those of us who were on the deck were starting to see some humour in this stand off. Two guys not giving an inch! Scruff was not letting up and Kurt just sat there. By now, many other people were coming out of their homes to see what all the noise was about.

Scruff had enough of yelling through a closed window, and now was a lot more pissed off. He yelled at Kurt to roll down the damn window. From where we were standing, we could see Kurt's window slowly being rolled down. He looked too scared to roll down the window at first, with this big, mad, scary fella at his door, but he rolled it down anyway as instructed.

Scruff didn't wait a second. As soon as the window was down, he put his head right inside the opening, but before he could even utter another word, Kurt punched Scruff right on the end of his nose. He then sped off leaving rubber on the pavement, and blood all over Scruff's face. The truck was long gone, and Scruff was left in the middle of the road bleeding. The laughing coming from all the people who were watching was as loud as the truck.

When Scruff made his way back to his deck, now madder than ever, all I could think of to say to him was, "Why the fuck did you lead with your face?" More laughter followed!

Scruff

10

TWO CARDINAL RULES
OF THE NORTH

November in Inuvik can get pretty darn cold…like almost parka cold. This time of year, everyone should have a bag of warm clothes and some survival gear whenever driving out of town, no matter how far down the Dempster Highway you're going. The North has some unique weather patterns. It can go from -8°C to -30°C in a very short time.

You can see for miles down the highway one minute, and be in a complete whiteout of swirling snow the next. It's a very harsh environment and not taken lightly by those who have lived there long enough to experience the wrath of Mother Nature. Lois and I both knew the right things to do, as Uncle was always talking about the right ways to be safe in case of breaking down, either by truck in the winter or by boat in the summer.

We woke up to a nice clear day with a bite of some cold mixed in. We were both looking forward to watching the semifinals of Canadian football later in the day. Wondering what to do until the game started, both of us decided that a quick drive down the highway would be fun. Maybe we would even shoot a ptarmigan or some rabbits to put in the freezer for much needed meals later.

The hunting for food was secondary today. We were just bored and wanted to get out while the weather was still in our favour.

We had decided to get going so that we could be back in plenty of time to watch the game. It started at 4pm and we left the house about 11am. I grabbed my 22 rifle in case we saw some game to put in the freezer along our way, and we hurried ourselves out of the door and into our big 1 ton 4x4 crew cab truck. We backed out of the driveway and started heading towards the highway.

It seems funny that when driving with no real destination in mind, other than a quick trip out of town, that no matter how far you plan to drive, you go farther and then farther. We managed to drive almost to the river crossing at Arctic Red (which is now known as Tsiigehtchic, and about 112km south of Inuvik).

There was no reason to go any further as we had a few rabbits and some ptarmigan in the back of the truck; plus the river crossings were closed, meaning no traffic was allowed on the ice, and the ferry that runs in summer was up out of the water and put away for winter. We had managed to slowly drive our way to within about 10km of the crossing before we decided it was time to turn around and head for home.

I got the truck sideways right in the middle of the road half way through my turn when the truck just quit. "How can that happen so fast?" I thought out loud. I tried to get it started with the key, but all the motor did was turn over and over. It would not start. On the drive to where we were broken down, we had not seen a single other vehicle, which, when you think about it…why would anyone be out here when that road crossing is still closed to traffic?

We tried everything that we knew and still couldn't find the problem with the truck, but we did notice that the temperature was dropping fast. It was downright cold now. And that's when we both noticed that we had not put our warm clothes in the truck as usual.

Lois was wearing running shoes and light travelling jacket. I also had runners on and a light jacket. Other than that, we had one bag of garbage in the back of the truck. You wonder why garbage is important? Well just as we were leaving the house a few hours earlier, Lois grabbed the bag and thought we could just take it out to the dump on the way home from our drive. Believe it or not, that garbage bag kept us warm for a little while. We opened the driver's door of the truck and put the garbage right on the road, and really close to the truck door, and burnt it for the warmth. Both of us were shivering and huddled together while it burned, until it was all gone. Then, I managed to find some willow in the ditches we could burn, but the snow was so deep that my feet and legs got pretty cold trudging back and forth.

We had made two very big mistakes that are now coming to light as we realize we can't walk anywhere. It's way too cold and we would freeze to death before too long. Plus, we realized that if we stayed here we would die from the cold. It was getting nasty cold out as we sat and thought about our two very big mistakes. We had broken the cardinal rules of the north.

13

Rule Number 1: Always dress for the elements. Take a bag of extra warm clothes, winter boots, matches, flares, extra safety items in your vehicle. Very important.

Rule Number 2: Always tell somebody where you are going and when you're coming back. Also, very important.

There are really only two solid rules for winter, and we broke both of them. We were out there alone and nobody even knew where we went. There were no cell phones, so we couldn't call AMA or even use the phone a friend method. We were getting worried, and wishing we had listened to Uncle Dick. We both thought we were going to die right in the middle of that road! If we had just followed two simple rules, we would not have had to worry, as someone would've come looking when we didn't come home within an hour of saying we would be back.

We had been stuck on the road for close to 3 hours at this point. It's hard to describe the pain from the cold. First, our feet were starting to hurt, then our hands. Lois and I were huddled in a hug as we both were uncontrollably shivering, which is never a good sign. We both knew that we may not get out of this alive.

There was still no sign of traffic, which we both knew wouldn't happen anyway. But, we did have hope, and that was about the extent of what we had...just hope!

It seemed like an eternity as we sat and hugged out our last moments together waiting for the quick and painful death that was coming for us. But wait…we could hear a vehicle and it was getting closer to us! It was coming from the way of the river crossing. How can that be possible? The river crossing was not safe to drive on yet. You had to be crazy to drive over that thin ice.

The vehicle pulled up to us and the person driving asked, "What

14

the hell are you doing blocking off the road?" They were not mad at us; they just wanted to be funny. They knew right away we were in trouble and needed some help. Turns out these guys were just making a booze run to Inuvik, then straight back to home at the river crossing. These Inuit fellas know the water and ice conditions better than anyone, so they took a chance on the ice.

That trip of theirs saved our lives; I have no doubt about that. They packed us into their vehicle, and we left the big blue truck right where it had stopped some 4 hours earlier. We were now bound for home by hope.

Like I said earlier, all we had was hope. Well, it came to us when we needed it the most!

Even as I write this story, which happened 34ish years ago, I can still feel how I felt in that cold truck. It is forever etched into my brain. Since that day, Lois and I always have a warm bag of clothes to take in the vehicle no matter how far we are going. Even though we have phones and can reach someone to come help, I'm sticking with Uncle's advice always from now on. We dodged a very big bullet that day!

TRUCK HAS A SLEEP OVER IN MACKENZIE PARKING LOT

It was a beautiful, warm and sunny spring Saturday in Inuvik; the perfect day to head on over to the Legion for opening time. On days like this you had to be on time or your spot up at the bar may be taken up by some other day drinker that just happened to drop in.

All of us regulars had our own special spot at the bar, and it was always the same. We also each had our own special drinking mug that we brought from our homes to drink from. The Legion was even nice enough to put hooks up in order to let all those mugs hang up above the bar, within reach of our special spots, of course.

Once I parked my truck in the parking lot, I hurried in to get my spot, my mug, and then a big drink to go in it.

During most Saturdays, the Saturdays that we had to spend in town anyway, there was always lots to do in the Legion. There were darts, shuffle board, pool, and then up at the bar you could jump into a fast-paced game of Liar's Dice. This game, if you lost, usually cost a bit of money to buy a round of drinks for the other's playing. You had to be the best liar, with a good poker face, in order to win.

Spending the day inside the Legion was not a hard thing to do at all. As a matter of fact, it felt more like a big party going on in your very own man cave. And, you didn't have to give away a bunch of booze and food to all these friends… so pretty nice in that regard.

The Legion was situated about a short two-minute walk from the Mackenzie Hotel (Mac)…or a four-minute stagger. That was perfect for us who liked to start drinking at the Legion and then head over to the Mac later. The drinks were a whole bunch cheaper in the Legion, and the crowd was not really into fighting or arguing. The Mackenzie, on the other hand, was full of people who loved to do both of those things.

Right across from the Legion, and within eyesight of the Mackenzie Hotel, was the RCMP building, jail and all…so walking back and forth from the Legion to the Mac was the smart thing to do. The RCMP could just look out their window and see both parking lots. It was slightly farther than a stone's throw away to each place.

After a full day of drinking and playing games in the Legion, a bunch of us decided it was time to head over to the Mackenzie. We usually did this walk/stagger around 11:00 pm, and bite the bullet on the higher whiskey prices. Plus, that's where the girls were.

On this Saturday, for some reason, I decided to drive my truck, instead of doing the walk thing. Once there, I parked way in the back corner of the parking lot. "I was being a responsible drunk," I thought at the time.

My truck

Once inside the Mac, the fun would begin. It was filling up quickly as everybody drank cheaper either at the Legion or at home first. With 11:00 pm being the magic hour, the bar would fill up quick.

The night was filled with the usual stuff. All in all, most nights played out the same, and we kind of liked it that way. After spending from 11:00 am to about 2:30 am drinking, we were usually pretty full.

This night, I just happened to stay back inside the bar talking with the owner, Walter "the Roofer", after everyone was gone. He was called that by everyone in town. When he came to Inuvik, he was a roofer contractor but turned into a bar owner. Walter and I talked and had a few extra drinks, on the house of course, but it was getting late and everyone had gone home. It was time for me to leave.

I made my way down the steps, stumbling a bit on most of them, while trying to find my truck keys in whatever pocket I had left them in. I had more than one pocket, so finding them was proving to be a tough task for me. It had been a very long day and night of partying. What can I say? I looked way over to the back of the empty parking lot where I had parked, and yay, my truck was there. I started towards it and about halfway there I found my keys. "How great is that," I was thinking. It was a pretty long walk home for me; driving was best at this point, I figured. There was hardly anybody out on the streets at this time, except the odd few walking about.

I managed to get myself to the truck and had just started to try and unlock the driver's door, when I felt a tap on my right shoulder. I quickly turned around as I thought a fight was coming, but instead I found myself looking straight at two RCMP officers. "Oh oh!"

With my keys in my hand and them both looking at me, the one officer said, "Hey Randy, you weren't thinking of getting in and driving your truck were you?"

I quickly answered that with these exact words. "No, Sir. I was just making sure it was all locked up before I walked home!"

He answered me with, "That's what we thought you were doing. Have a nice walk."

Did I mention that it was a very long walk home. I saw those two officers at least four times as I walked home. They were either making sure I got home, or they were just making sure I didn't double back to go get the truck. I prefer to think they kept me safe from driving, and safe while walking home. Inuvik was not the best place for a guy walking alone in the wee hours. Anything could happen!

After that encounter and not getting arrested for drunk driving, I had a better understanding of how good our RCMP members could be to us. I changed everything when I drank from that day forward. Yep, I learned my lesson the easy way.

OUR POSSESSED CAT

I can't help myself; I just have to write this story. It has been on my mind since I decided I needed to write a book. So here it is.

Brian P. was our forever roommate. Lois and I both had a blast with him. He was fun to be around. He was pretty good at staging practical jokes. I liked drinking, so did he. I loved boating, so did he. I rode my motorcycle in motocross racing, and he watched!

I am not sure when we got our first pet, and I am equally not sure why we got our first pet. But there it was one day, our new cat, living right inside our trailer. I have always been kind of partial to dogs. I love dogs. Dogs can go outside to shit and piss. I liked that part. Cats, on the other hand, do their crapping and pissing wherever you put the litter box. We quickly figured out that this cat, over the course of the first month, was trying to be the boss of the entire house, and it seemed to be working.

If it shit on the floor in front of the television, when we were watching something, we cleaned it up. This cat was smart. He would just walk away from the mess behind him with a smirk on his face. That was really starting to piss me off.

Then this started at night. Soon after Lois and I went to our room and Brian P. to his room, the noise would start. Not your normal night time noise, more like stuff-being-thrown-to-the-floor-in-the-kitchen-type noise.

When it first happened, Lois and I both jumped out of bed and ran down the hallway, past Brian P.'s bedroom, and into the kitchen. Right there, in front of the fridge on the floor, was a bunch of pencils, pens, and various other small crap that is usually in the cup on top of the fridge. Okay, maybe somebody put the stuff too close to the edge, and it somehow fell to the floor. There was no explanation that we could come up with, so we cleaned up the mess then went back to bed.

The very next night, we had only been in bed ten minutes, and again, a crashing noise from the kitchen. We both jumped out of bed and headed for the kitchen to see everything that was on top of the fridge was now all over the floor, in front of the fridge, again! What the hell was going on here? We were cleaning this mess up and we still had no idea of what happened. Something pretty strange was going on, and it was pissing us off while keeping us awake at night.

Then, a light bulb went on in my head. "Where is that fucking cat?" I said aloud. Lois and I both started looking and couldn't find it. We went back to our bedroom, but this time when I closed the door, I kept it open a little bit so that I could see the fridge. It didn't take very long before I saw the cat sneaking into the kitchen. He jumped up on to the chair, then jumped up onto the kitchen table, and from there he jumped right on to the top of the fridge. Bingo…now the mystery noise was solved. Meanwhile, the cat was batting his paws into the stuff on the fridge, until it all hit the floor one more time. I let it happen, for now!

Then, the wheels were turning inside my head. I was making a plan that would stop this night time ritual this demon cat had.

While I was at work the next day, I couldn't help but try and think of ways to put a stop to this witch cat's game. I was usually pretty quick at thinking shit like this up, but this one was tough on my brain. I wasn't dealing with just any cat. We had a possessed cat in the trailer. I may not be proud of what I felt I needed to do to teach that devil cat a lesson, but nonetheless, it had to be this way.

My plan went into effect the minute I got home from work. Lois tried to talk me out of it, but I was not listening. I was already in too deep. I had to get things set up for the night. The first thing I did was grab some clear tape, the kind you can just pull out and then cut it on those little plastic teeth thingies. Wrapping presents type of tape…Scotch tape! I had grabbed a small handful of ordinary small tacks from work, just before leaving for the day. I had all I needed now.

I got up on the chair and pulled four strips of tape about eight inches in length off that roll. I then pushed the little pointy end of the tacks through each of the pieces of tape, spaced about every half inch. I then moved all the little things that belonged up on the fridge, not on the floor as the cat thought, just a bit back from where they normally would have been. I then took those four strips of tape and stuck them to the top of the fridge with the little pointy ends sticking up.

The trap was set. Now, we just needed to wait until bedtime and see who the boss was here: cat or human? To some of you who may think tacks are a bit much, remember when back in school, when we were young, somebody would put a tack on your school desk seat as a joke? Sure, it hurt a little, but only for a second.

The three of us were sitting around having a few drinks, bull shitting about all things important, like this damn cat that has been running the house like he owned it. Bedtime could not come quick enough for me as this cat needed a wakeup call, and I was going to deliver that message my way. Talking to it had failed miserably. 10:30 pm…bedtime. We all retired to our rooms for the night and laid in bed waiting. It seemed like forever, but then it started!

As I said earlier, I had witnessed how the cat was getting up that high on the fridge. I can now picture in my mind each and every noise it took for the cat to reach the fridge and its night time toys. First, we heard the quiet little sound of his paws hitting the chair, then a brief rest. Next, came the unmistakable sound of his tiny paws landing on the table top. I am now shivering with excitement. I'm having to suppress the urge to open the bedroom door just a wee bit, so that I can watch the next step…the all-important lesson step!

Then, it happened. We heard the third and final jump up onto the fridge full of those tacks. Instantly, the cat let out some very surprised and shocked kind of cat-like noises, not your regular meow here, more of a loud "WTF!" in our language. The next noise, which was a mere instant after landing on the fridge, was the noise of the cat landing on the floor, not his normal dismount! We all came running out of our rooms and met at the fridge. The first thing we noticed was that all the things that were on the fridge were still on the fridge. The second thing we saw was little, tiny droplets of blood on the floor right where the cat had landed.

We now had a tiny blood trail to follow. We find the cat and he is up underneath the arm chair where nobody would have ever found him. He was just staring at us and licking his little paws, which were not seriously damaged, maybe a bit sore. Mostly, I think his pride was hurt worse this go round, but we had stopped that insane, possessed, demonic cat from jumping on that fridge ever again. Mission accomplished!

Scotty with Uncle Dick's dog, Lightning. I love dogs!

HELICOPTER AND TRIKES

I know I will get myself into a whole lot of trouble writing about this from my wife. We were not yet married, so I am willing to take one for the team, and go ahead and tell what happened to us one weekend while camping down the Dempster highway.

In the early part of the summer, the lake we usually boat to still has ice on it, so we usually take advantage of the warmer days to just head out to go camp in tents, and bask away in the sun, while drinking the days and nights away at a nice little spot called Caribou Creek.

We were just sitting around the campfire on a Saturday afternoon telling stories while sipping on a few drinks. We were enjoying the sunshine and the good company when a couple of our buddies showed up with their Honda trikes. Now up to this day, I had never ridden one and when they were driving around in and out of the creek, up the banks, down the road, and just about anywhere they wanted to go, I needed to give it a try!

I managed to talk them into letting my wife-to-be and I take those two red Hondas for a rip. Perfect! I was thinking, "Now, if we could get far enough away from camp so the two of us could get naked"…oh my mind was thinking how much fun this was going to be. I could only hope that she was thinking the same thing I was thinking…some naked fun under the sun.

After a quick orientation on how to drive these things from our buddies, off we went, with me in the lead. It was my intention to quickly get somewhere where nobody could see us and get her naked. Well, it didn't take very long to figure out that "getting to that quickly" was not going to happen. I was driving way faster than she was, but in her defense there was no trail. The tundra is not the easiest thing to try to drive a 3 wheel trike across. I found myself stopping and walking back to where she was stuck, and helping her to get going again. This process happened way too many times for my liking, but I sucked it up, and kept helping her. I still had visions in my head of what was going to happen once we found just the right spot.

We had been struggling along for about a half hour when there it was…a pretty good size chunk of water, just like a dugout in the middle of gravel quarry. We parked the machines and right away it looked like my plan was starting to work as she got off her machine, and practically jumped right out of her clothes, before I was even off my trike. I could see that I was falling behind for a change, so off the machine I went while trying to get rid of my clothes as quickly as she had done.

Once I managed to get out of my clothes, I looked over to see Lois already in the water and having a great time splashing around. She was calling out my name and asking me join her in the water.

This is a good time to tell you that I am scared shitless of water! I can't swim at all, and I found myself running up and down the water's edge. It is safe to say I must have looked rather silly to say the least. She knew I couldn't swim, so I guess she was enjoying watching me act like a lost little hungry and horny pup.

She continued to swim back and forth egging me on to get in. Hell, she even stood up once with her boobs visible. I was wishing I had taken those swimming lessons my mom and dad said I should take.

It was hot day, and it took a lot of begging on my part to finally get her out of that water and back on dry land. She really seemed to be enjoying the begging part! But I had other ideas that I would enjoy more. It took some convincing, but I managed to talk her into sitting on my lap facing me while I drove my borrowed trike around at a slow pace so we could enjoy some "piece" and quiet. Finally, my plan was working, what more can a guy ask for when he has a naked girl sitting on his lap while on a trike in the middle of nowhere?

After doing a little drive around, I figured it was time to stop the machine and see what position we could try next. I shut the machine off and that's when we both heard a helicopter. It was right above us, and I could see both guys looking down at us grinning from ear to ear. My wife-to-be just covered her face and leaned into my chest covering herself. We both just sat there on the trike with me looking straight up at those guys. I did what any normal guy would do in this situation. I gave them the thumbs up signal with both hands to say all is good here. They flew off after going around in a circle above us, and we got to finishing what we had started with our eyes glued to the skies.

On the trip back to camp, I didn't help her near as much as I had on the trip in, not because I am not a gentleman, but she did tease me at the water's edge for a little longer than I wanted. To think, she still married me anyway!

As I write this, I can't help but wonder what story those guys in the chopper tell their friends about that day.

Lois with the trikes.

LOIS' FIRST TRIP TO YA YA LAKE

Living in Inuvik could be a lot of fun, or no fun at all, depending on what you had to do keep you busy. Some people living in town didn't do much other than go to work, go home, and maybe have people over for some much-needed company. We did other things. We did have some choices other than just staying home.

Life was different way up north. We didn't get much summer, and when we did, we had 24 hours of daylight for those few short summer months. Then, after summer, we went straight to winter. There was no fall to speak of. We had three seasons we could count on: long winter, short spring, and short summer. The locals used to talk about the seasons as ten months of winter and two months of poor dog sledding.

30

This part of the world was not for everybody. If you came up to Inuvik, you usually liked everything about the place, or you could hardly wait to get out of there and back to where you came from. Some people just didn't give it much of a chance or have an open mind, I guess. If you tried, you could always find something to do in any of the three seasons.

I must admit I fell in love with the place as soon as I first arrived in town as a young and dumb kid running away from problems back home. But things were a bit different for me in Inuvik. I had family up there, and that was what kept me sane… out of trouble, not so much!

My Uncle Dick and Aunt Lucy were a huge reason I enjoyed Inuvik as much as I did. They took care of me, introduced me to their many friends in town, and basically tried to keep me out of any trouble. I can't say enough about these two. My aunt is my dad's sister, and I know she struggled for a long time being that far north away from her family back in Manitoba. In those days, it was a very big world and people didn't travel very far. Inuvik seemed like it was at the end of the world in the 1960s and 70s.

There was not much that Uncle loved more than going to his cabin out on Ya Ya Lake. The 90-mile boat ride itself was an adventure. Getting there without blowing up a motor or hitting a mud bar and being stuck for hours, and the big choppy water, were just a few of the problems we encountered. So yeah, we had seen it all. Each summer brought some of the same troubles, as well as new challenges, when we made our way out to the cabin.

I remember when Lois, who was my girlfriend at the time, came on one of those trips to the cabin for the very first time. It was a beautiful day to be boating. The river was very calm, and the wind was not a factor in the day's travels, which was always a good thing. We were moving along at about thirty miles an hour, so it was about three hours to get to the cabin from town, if all went well.

Uncle Dick's prized green boat.

Uncle Dick really loved his big green boat. You could fit six to eight people and all their gear for a weekend in it, and still get there in three hours, most of the time! Uncle, in all the trips I was on with him, never once let anybody drive his prize possession… not once ever!

On this trip, there was Uncle, Aunty, their daughter, and Brian P. and his girlfriend, Lois, myself and all our gear to get us through a fun weekend at the cabin. We were all excited as it was easy boating. We had a new person coming along, and we were all drinking happily. Uncle liked having new people on board. He enjoyed showing them the sites along the river. He made a very good guide, and if I was to ever break down or get lost, he would be the guy I would want with me.

To this day I have no idea why Uncle said, "Hey Randy, come up and take over the wheel for a bit. I have got to check on something." Now hold on here, did I not just say that Uncle never ever let anyone drive his boat...ever!? Well, it didn't take me long to get into position to take over the controls. I was told just keep the nose of the boat pointed right at the marker buoy way off in the distance.

The marker buoys were for the big barges to travel, and they were placed every year along the deepest part of the river. If you got outside the lane between them, you would find yourself stuck tight in mud that wouldn't let go.

I was thinking that Uncle wanted me to drive the boat so that I could maybe impress my new girlfriend with my boating skills. Yet Uncle and I both knew I did not have that skill. Anyway, once I got all the quick instructions and a fresh drink to put in the little holder by the throttle, I sat my ass in the captain's seat for the very first time.

I'm not sure what happened or why it happened so fast. When my ass hit the chair and my hands got on the wheel, there instantly came a very loud bang, some clanging, and the motor just plain stopped dead right out in the middle of the river.

The next few minutes were critical and chaotic. Uncle yelled, "Point the boat to shore, Randy. Brian P., grab that jerry can of gas. I'll grab the line to tie the boat up on shore," he said. Then, he started with more instructions. "Lois get something, anything at all you can find to burn...get a damn smudge going as the mosquitoes will drive us crazy on shore."

Ah, yes, the mosquito season up north was in full mode. They would literally drive a person insane. They come in big clouds and are in your face...millions of the bastards! Not even little ones. Great big ones that leave you itching for hours. I can't stress enough how bad they were. If you were in a slow fishing boat on that river, those mosquitoes could keep up and drive you crazy.

Once all the chores that Uncle had been giving out to us had been done, and the fire smudge was going strong, we were all instructed to stand right beside the fire. The smudge smoke was engulfing each of us. It was pure magic, as long as we stood right in the middle of that smoke. Now that the chaos was starting to slow down, we all had a chance to grab a well-deserved drink. We needed to assess our situation.

First thing to do was to find out what happened. How much shit we were in, I guess, is a better way of putting it. What had happened? Five minutes earlier, Uncle was driving along and all he did was let me drive, and now here we stand in the land of the mosquitoes and a big smudge.

While we were all huddled around the smudge, Uncle went over to the boat to have a quick look to see what caused the big bang and clang. It didn't take him long to spot our trouble. There was a big hole in the side of the motor, a pretty big hole I might add! We knew it could not be fixed with mechanic's wire and gum; we needed a tow back to town. Uncle didn't seem too worried about our troubles at all. Actually, we were all quite okay as long as we stayed inside the smoke.

For some strange reason this Friday, we were the first of many boats to leave town heading to the cabin. There was one rule that, no matter what, was always done the same way. There was only one satellite phone between the 5-6 boats of people going to the lake on any given weekend. The last boat out of town was the boat that the phone was in, so that if anybody broke down, they would know help was not too far behind and they would have a phone. There was no AMA on the river, so we relied on each other for help.

We had not been waiting long when we could see off in the distance a couple of the other boats heading our way. Once they got to us, we saw how full their boats were already. We figured they had no room for any of us, let alone the gear we had. That was not going to be a problem, as they told us that Frank and Marie were coming along in a short time. We pushed their boats back out into the open water, and told them we would see them in a while…hopefully!

Somehow Uncle had this quiet calm about him whenever there was trouble, and tonight was no different. We all felt safe, had some drinks, talked, and laughed about my boat breaking ability as we waited for the last boat. As luck would have it, it wasn't long before we could see help coming our way.…it was Frank and Marie. They had the phone we so desperately needed, as well as a ride! When they pulled in right beside our broken boat and realized this boat was going nowhere tonight, they offered up some room in their boat.

Uncle did all the figuring, and came to the conclusion that Brian P. and his girlfriend, along with Aunt Lucy and most of our gear could fit in Frank's boat. We all went about moving things around as quickly as possible. Remember the mosquitoes were killers. We would have put a Nascar pit crew to shame with how fast we had them loaded up and pushed off shore to continue on to the cabin without us.

Now all that was left on shore was Uncle and his daughter, and Lois and me. We now had the phone, which was super important. In the harsh environments of the north, even in summer, things were tough!

Uncle tried calling all the local airplane companies in Inuvik that had float planes, so that somebody could come and pick us up and fly us to the cabin. Most of these planes were tight fitting, room for four as long as you squished in a bit.

He was having no luck at all. Nobody was answering the phone, but then again this was late at night, like 11:00 pm late. Okay, so now we can't call anybody for a ride. But, Uncle's son was working in the Mackenzie hotel that night as a bouncer. I should have been with him, as we both looked after that place on weekend nights for the owners, Walter and Hildegard. (That's a bunch of other stories though, which we will get to later.)

It only took one call to the bar and get his son on the line. Uncle asked him if he could see any pilots sitting in the bar. Perhaps a strange question this late at night, but most people were in that bar. It took a few minutes of waiting before yes was the answer. He had found one. "Is he sober enough to fly?" was the next question Uncle asked. After a minute or two of him talking with the pilot, while the music in the background made it hard to actually talk to each other, it was agreed that he was fine to fly and would come get us. Help is coming. Yay!

We kept that big smudge going so that the pilot would see us from the air for miles. Remember, the sun is up 24 hours in the summer. You could see for miles and miles night and day. It wasn't long before we could hear the plane coming. Time for the happy dance! We would soon be on our way to the cabin to meet up with all those that went on ahead of us.

The plane landed out in the river and taxied up to our makeshift camp. We were excited and happy that we could now leave those pesky, huge blood-sucking mosquitoes behind. We loaded up the little amount of gear we had left. Lois and I and Uncle's daughter squished into the two seats in the back and Uncle sat up front with the pilot. The pilot asked where we were going.

We were so excited to be inside, and those mosquitoes outside, and to be headed to the cabin to join the party, that we didn't notice the obvious thing. Uncle asked the pilot if he knew the way to Ya Ya lakes. The pilot said, "Yeah. He had flown past our cabin before."

We taxied out into the middle of the river channel. The pilot was getting up to take-off speed and all was good. After reaching that magic little speed that gets these float planes out of the water, up we went. Then, suddenly, we came crashing back down, hard, and the plane just stopped dead. The pilot hit his head on the dash and his words were slurred when he said, "Oops, sorry everyone."

That was when we noticed the obvious thing. Our pilot was drunk as shit. Uncle shot him that look that only Uncle could do. I could see how mad he was and then he said, "You want me to fly this damn thing? You're drunk!"

The pilot said, "What were you expecting? I was in the bar when you called…and here I am, so just let me fly you guys to the cabin now". This guy was making Uncle angry. The more he spoke the more pissed off Uncle became.

It was a tense inside that tiny plane, and it remained that way for the whole trip. Once we were finally up in the air, things were going well, and we were back to having a drink. It should only be about a twenty-minute flight to the cabin. I have to say, we usually flew with the same couple of pilots from town. This was our first trip with this pilot. As he was flying along, Uncle said to the pilot, "Thought you said you knew where my cabin is?"

"Of course I do. I'm heading straight for it."

Uncle, without missing a beat, says to him, "No, you're not. You're heading to Tuk. My cabin is way over that way," as he pointed across the skyline in a totally different direction. Tuk was on the shore of the Beaufort Sea…miles from the cabin!

That conversation turned into an argument between Uncle and the drunk pilot. Trying to tell a drunk pilot he is wrong doesn't really go over very well. Some of them, and only some, think, because they could fly float planes, that they were much better than us mere ground walkers.

Uncle was getting nowhere with this directionally challenged, drunk idiot, so he just quit trying. He joined the three of us for a drink instead. Us back seat people never spoke a word about any of this...Uncle could handle anything. We were good.

We had been up in the air for about twenty minutes and, all of a sudden, we look down and there is the community of Tuk (houses everywhere down there) and the Beaufort Sea ahead of us. That's when Uncle turned, stared at that drunken pilot and said, in the most scary tone of voice that I have never heard, "Okay, asshole, which one of those houses is my fucking cabin?" The pilot never said a word as Uncle pointed in the opposite direction and said to him, "Fly that way now, you fucking idiot."

Uncle Dick's cabin at Ya Ya Lake.

From what we heard in the coming days, that pilot was sent back south to dry out. That made all of us who relied on this mode of transportation from time to time ecstatic. We did make it to the cabin obviously, but the pilot was quiet the rest of the trip.

Even after all that had happened that night, Lois still enjoyed her very first trip to Ya Ya Lake.

VOLUNTEER BOUNCERS

The Mackenzie Hotel was nicknamed "the Zoo" for good reason. Sometimes the people inside turned into animals. Booze has that effect on some, especially during the very long winter months of severe cold and mostly dark days and nights. I know most towns down south had their own style of bar nicknamed "the Zoo". I have seen the insides of a few of those during my drinking career in Brandon, Manitoba, and surrounding area. None of those would even come close to "the Zoo" in Inuvik.

I happened to be good friends with Walter, the owner of the Mackenzie Hotel. He was a big soft-spoken man, a very giving fella with a great sense of humour. Most everyone who met this man liked him right away. I knew Walter and his wife, Hildegard, through my Uncle Dick, who had introduced us while I was living the dream in Inuvik. As Walter and I became friends, I found out quickly that there was absolutely nothing I could do that would get me barred or thrown out...nothing!

Matter of fact, if I walked in and Walter was standing at his usual spot by the bar, he would act surprised to see me and say, "Hey Randy…Schnapps?" And of course, "no" was the wrong answer every time.

Walter stood there most nights, overlooking the crowd, and trying to keep the patrons under control, which was a chore during the weekends.

The Mackenzie Hotel had three separate bars inside the building. When you first walked into the bar, you were in the Brass Rail, a place to have a peaceful drink, or supper. It was the quiet one of the three bars. After you went through the Brass Rail, you ended up in the much bigger bar known as "the Zoo", with a band playing music and lots of drinking, dancing, and fighting inside there. And saving the worst for last, if you went through the back door of "the Zoo", you were now in the games room known as "the Pub". Pool, shuffle board, and some crazy shit happened inside there. I will get to that in another story.

This was really the "go-to place" for all your needs. Dancing, food, drinks, games, fighting, and practical jokes were the normal night activities.

Things were really starting to get busy in Inuvik, and with that came more and more people, which brought more drinkers into Walter's place. He was having trouble trying to keep the new arrivals from getting into fights with the locals. Soon every night was a fighting night. With Walter getting swamped every night with problems in one, or all three, of the bars within his building, he decided to hire some bouncers from down south and bring them up to help. These guys were big guys, and I say guys (with an s) as over a stretch of a month or so, he hired four different fellows to come up and try to help.

The first guy who came from Edmonton was working his

second night, which was a Saturday. I guess he must have pissed off a few local boys who grew up in Inuvik, because after his shift ended, there were six of those town guys waiting for him outside. The short story is they broke his legs and told him to get out of town. He did just that after his hospital visit. He lasted only two nights. Walter needed help again. Without going into detail, the three other guys faced the very same type of injuries and were sent packing. The local guys really didn't like the attitude of big city bouncers in "the Zoo".

I guess the word was out in the bouncer's community in the south not to go to Inuvik. If they sent a tougher guy up, the local guys just took them down with more of their friends. Things were getting out of control on weekends at "the Zoo".

On one Saturday night, it was business as usual. It was busy in all three bars, but no bouncers to be seen. This was like a green light for the rowdies, and more guys were acting up and getting away with it. Walter was only one man, and he was past the point of trying to get involved in throwing anybody out. I was in the bar on this Saturday night with a few friends and my cousin, who had lived in Inuvik his whole life.

Walking amongst the crowd of people you could feel the tension rising as we neared closing time, and time for everyone to get out. There had been a few little scraps here and there throughout the night, but nothing that didn't work itself out.

Some nights the bar just empties itself. Some go home, some go outside to scrap, then the rest go to watch. Easy night when that would happen. But this night was proving to be too much for Walter to handle. He came over to me and asked if I could help get a table of six local regulars to leave. They still had maybe eight full drinks, and they had no intention to leave until they finished those last few. These were some of the guys who had sent our imported bouncers back south. Walter was getting worried about that, but he knew me well and knew I could handle myself in these situations.

I hung out there lots and I had judo and karate on my side. The local guys knew me. I was 140 pounds, fast on the punch and quicker on the kicks. I had fought up to four guys at one time with no help, and had them all on the floor in a very short time. That's why Walter asked for my help.

I looked over at the table and the six of them were laughing and having a drunken old time. I watched for a couple minutes, so that I could find out who their main man was in that group. Once I had all I needed to know, I asked my cousin, Harry, to go over to the main doors and get ready. He did just that, as I walked in the direction of the table. I stood right at the table and politely asked them to leave as it's way past closing time, and Walter wanted to go home to bed. Imagine my surprise when they look up at me and tell me to fuck off. They are not done yet. I was expecting that, given who they were.

Again, I asked, "Please guys, just leave and come back another day." "Fuck off" was my answer once again. Out of the corner of my eye I can see my cousin standing inside the front door, and I was pretty much done with being nice to these assholes now. Without even giving them another warning, I swiped my hand across the table where a full drink was and it hit the guy on my left in the head. Before they could react, I grabbed the leader of the pack's head and slammed it into the table knocking him out. I grabbed him by his shirt and belt, and started dragging him towards the front door while yelling at Harry, "Open the door! Open the door!"

Outside that door was a set of four or five stairs leading down into the gravel parking lot. When I got to the top of those stairs, I threw the guy right into the parking lot and went back in to get the others. The other five guys were still at the table. The one who had some cuts on his head didn't want to leave yet. I punched another so hard on his nose that blood spewed everywhere, then grabbed another guy and headed for the door. The rest now followed, as I threw him down those stairs. After that was done, I walked back inside the bar to see it empty, except for Walter, Harry and myself. Walter's eyes were big with excitement as he started pouring three schnapps. He says, "Damn, that looked like fun for you guys. Those six were part of the group that attacked the four other bouncers and sent them home broken up."

"Really," I said, "it didn't seem too hard to get them to leave. I only had to throw two of them down those stairs and the rest went running."

That was the first of many nights helping Walter. We were paid very well for our services. Free drinks any day, all day was all we asked for. It didn't take long for word to get out that there were two new bouncers… my cousin, Harry, and myself. We had the same troubles the other guys had, but there was two of us and we worked well together. The scrappers would try to separate us, so that they stood a chance of winning a fight. We tried not to let that happen, as it would be trouble for us individually. That's in their nature though, like a pack of wolves circling their food, sort of!

I didn't know it at the time that the local bar crowd had given me a nickname. Over the course of a few weeks they were noticing that I never backed away from anybody, and was always ready to defend myself or my friends, including Walter and the Mackenzie. The night I found out my nickname was after bar closing and Harry was already off to some party. Things were under control, and I would be leaving shortly. I said good night to Walter and thanked him for the drinks once again. (I did that a lot!)

It was around 2:30 am when I walked out to the front lobby only to be greeted by those original guys full of liquor and wanting a fight. My first thought was, "Damn, I wish Harry was here." They had us separated as they planned out in advance. I walked towards them without blinking an eye; adrenalin was running through my whole body.

Here in front of me were the tough guys from town, in a group. One of them alone would have been a cake walk for me, but there were six, and they liked breaking legs and arms so that you couldn't fight back. As I got closer to them, they started to put themselves in a circle with me in the middle. I was totally surrounded. That's how they fight. It was a tough spot to be in. I may not win this one. I told the ringleader to stand aside as I was headed to my truck to home. He said, "No."

I asked, "How is this going to play out, one at a time or do I have to fight you all at once?"

"You're going to get messed up like we did to the others," he announced quite firmly. "Alright," I'm thinking, "he will go down first as before, then I'll turn and swift kick the guy standing behind me, and then hope to see a few running after that." But just before I could put this plan in motion, the front door opens and in walks one of their own. Now, I have seven guys and just me! I am quickly rethinking my plan as this seventh guy was tough.

This guy begins to talk and he says to the others, "Hey, leave this guy alone. He's that crazy white fucker." That's when I knew I had a name, and that alone got me out of a sure beat down. They liked to fight the white guys, but they didn't want anything to do with a white guy who was crazy and not scared of much.

45

I never, ever got hurt and neither did my cousin Harry, and that made Walter a very happy man. They left me alone after that, and clearing the bar was easier for us.

JUST FOLLOW ME, CHARLIE

When I first met Charlie, it was in the Legion (big surprise there). I met most of my friends in that building. Charlie was not a drinker of any booze whatsoever when I met him, but I guess before that he knew his way around a few bottles of whatever was available at the time.

It was getting close to springtime in Inuvik, and that draws a lot of people out from their homes to get ready for the short summer that will soon be there. Those of us who were lucky enough to have a place out in the delta within boating distance were getting excited about the summer ahead. Most important during this time was getting the boat fixed up from any of the last summer's disasters that we had encountered. This was mostly standing at the bar in the Legion and talking about those times…reliving them was always fun!

I didn't know it at the time, but meeting Charlie turned out to be the beginning of a lifelong friendship. Inuvik had a way of bringing folks together, as everyone looked after their neighbours and friends alike. People were friendly and always willing to lend a hand either for free or we used the barter system for many different things that a person may need.

Charlie turned out to be a handy guy to know. He could fix most anything and kept himself busy helping others whenever possible with his many talents. He could play any instrument you put in front of him. He could sing and write a song in a matter of minutes. He was also a good poet…he was a true-blue Newfoundlander! He could entertain a crowd for hours with a guitar in his hands, or a harmonica, or an accordion, and many other instruments.

But best of all, he had his own boat. It was a 15-foot tri-hull that had a 115 hp mercury motor on the back. I was thinking that it was going to be fast on the water, but I never thought 60mph was fast until I witnessed it on the Mackenzie River.

Charlie had been using his boat just around the Inuvik area and only venturing out to Airport Lake on weekends, where some friends had cabins set up. We became close friends in a hurry. Hell, he even lived at the end of our street with his family.

It was during one of our many visits to the Legion that I introduced Charlie to Uncle Dick. We were talking about the upcoming boating season and Charlie got pretty excited when Uncle and I were talking about going to Ya Ya Lake. He was asking all kinds of questions like, "How much gas does it take to get there and back? What about sandbars? How far is it?" and "What about fishing?" Charlie was full of these kinds of questions. Uncle told him to just come on up anytime he wanted, after the ice was all gone, of course.

That made Charlie a happy guy. He was going to be able to

take his boat 90 miles one way and have some new adventures, but he was really worried about finding his way. It was not an easy task to get there! I told Charlie that I knew the way. I had driven the boat up there many times. "Next time we go," I said, "just follow me…I know the way!"

Summer way up north can never come soon enough for those of us that loved boating more than riding snowmobile for 10 months of the year. But nevertheless, it does show up every single year. This summer was going to be a fun-filled summer of boating every single weekend that we could. Weather was a big factor in deciding if and when we could get on the river. If the wind was coming in wrong, we were stuck on shore, plus we had some big bodies of water to cross. Let me say right here, that's not fun boating if you get caught halfway across that water especially in an open boat, no top, nothing but water hitting you in the face and watering down our drinks at the same time. Horrible that was!

The day had finally arrived that we were going to Ya Ya Lakes. The ice was off of the lake; the river was calm…everything was a go! Charlie was taking his boat. Lois and I had our boat with our son Scotty, as well as Charlie's son, Ron, and Uncle Dick had his boat, "the green machine." That's what others in town and throughout the delta named that big boat.

Charlie was all anxious and nervous about the trip, having never covered that many miles in the harsh delta landscapes and different little channels leading to nowhere. Again, I reassured him that as long as he stayed right behind my boat, we would have no problems at all. I couldn't stress enough that he needed to be right behind me. If you miss a channel by a couple of feet in either direction, it could spell disaster and put you high and dry on a mud bar. "Never fun when that happens," I told him.

Uncle Dick was out front leading the way with me behind him and Charlie right on my ass. He was taking this trip with extreme caution and staying so close to us we could actually talk to him… okay, maybe a bit of a yell back and forth. The sun was high in the sky, the river was perfect, and we were having a good trip.

Remember when I said that little boat of Charlie's was fast? Well, my boat totally filled to capacity could do 30mph…a pretty good clip on water with a full boat. Charlie decided that he wanted to show off that 60mph boat of his. He went out and around me and then continued to drive circles around me while I was at top speed…that ass. He was right. That little white boat was flying around us faster than the mosquitoes could.

After a few times circling us, I motioned for him to get back behind me as we were coming up to a difficult part of the river known for those damn mud bars. I didn't really want to have to try and pull him out of that mud should he get into it. The mud is really sticky in the river, meaning if you're stuck, you're really stuck!

This bad spot was about 15 miles from the cabin. Then there was one nastier spot left to go. After that, we all could let our guards down a bit and enjoy the last leg, drinking heavily. Charlie must have thought by now that I did know the river well, and believing me when I said I would get him to the cabin safe and happy, as he was still right behind our boat.

I think I let my guard down maybe a wee bit too soon and I asked for another rye and coke. I was cruising at 30mph. Uncle was way up in front somewhere, and Charlie was right where I told him to be, behind my boat, almost too close! My drink was still fresh in my hands when all hell broke loose.

We came to a very quick, sudden stop. We were well onto the mud bar. My drink hit the windshield, my head hit the steering

50

wheel, and most of the items in our boat moved around to different spots. I was dazed a bit when I looked over the side of the boat. We were in deep mud, and Charlie was in right behind me…both of us stuck tight like a couple of mice on a glue trap.

Uncle Dick soon realized we were not behind him and came back to where he found the both of us. Lots of laughing was going on now. My head had a big old nasty bump on it and my windshield was full of whiskey…so yeah, maybe it looked funny to the people from a boat that was still in the water. Uncle tied onto Charlie's boat and got him pulled out, but my boat was totally stuck. We had a hell of a time trying to pull it this way and that way. Nothing was working very well for us.

Finally, Charlie tied on to my boat and pulled with his boat, while I was outside of the boat wearing my hip waders, pushing and lifting as he pulled. This seemed to be working, as ever so slowly the water was getting higher on my waders and the mud was letting go of my boat. It wasn't even a minute later that off the mud it came, with me still hanging on the edge of the boat. I was now running on the water as Charlie continued to drag me further out into the middle. Like I said before, I can't swim. I can't even dog paddle, and everyone knew that. So out of shear fear, I managed to hold on long enough to kick one leg up and over the side of the boat, while everyone was laughing at me, including Uncle and my wife!

Once I was back inside my boat, Charlie quit pulling and we all got our shit together for the rest of the way to the cabin. We made it safe and sound even after all that mess I got us into. We unloaded all the stuff from the boats and went inside for some party time at the lake.

Finally, Charlie got to see the beauty of Ya Ya Lake. His first trip was memorable to say the least. He was so happy to be sitting inside the cabin 90 miles from Inuvik, he pulled out his guitar and wrote this song in under a half hour for us. Here it is word for word:

SKIPPER RANDY DAY

We left Inuvik in a raging calm;
We must make Ya Ya before the sun goes down.
To be true I knew not the way,
"Just follow me," said Randy Day.

So right behind his boat I go,
to Timbuktu for all I know.
For trust I must, I knew not the way,
put all my faith in Randy Day.

Half hour past I see a sign,
Inuvik is 15 miles behind.
I'm sure we're going the right way,
I'll not lose sight of Randy Day.

Reindeer Station we'll pass up ahead,
but a left turn is taken instead.
I begin to doubt if this was the way,
but there's no choice now but to follow Randy Day.

Ten minutes later we pull to the shore,
a piss break is all and my bladder was sore.
Then it's out to the rough water that's in the way,
and breaking the trail was Randy Day.

A rough ride it was till we passed Bar C,
then we all pulled over for another pee.
He got us this far he must know the way,
I sure do respect Mr. Randy Day.

Then it's off to the last leg of our trip,
after this run one could use a nip.
Ya Ya's now not far away
and I was led by the best, Mr. Randy Day.

Second Creek to the right and we're home free,
the boat up ahead I will follow with glee.
I should apologize for doubting his way,
for there's no skipper better than Captain Randy Day.

Then all of a sudden there was a terrible fright,
we were high on a mud bank and held in tight.
What I fool I've been to follow his way,
what an <u>asshole,</u> this Randy Day.

Written by my friend, Charles Ryan (Charlie) pictured below.

NEW YEAR'S EVE PARTY AT GUY'S

New Year's in Inuvik is much the same as anywhere: parties going on all over town and drinking people trying to get to as many parties as possible. This New Year's Eve, the party we were headed to was at our good friend Guy's apartment.

Guy had the best parties! Lots of people coming and going, lots of really good food, and lots to drink. Great drawing cards to a successful party with laughs, drunk fun, and sometimes even the police would show up!

Lois and I went to the party early. I liked being early to any party. Brian P., our roommate, was with us. Scruff, our good friend, was also with us. I think, over the course of the night, most of Inuvik had come through the place. The night was going great, and everyone was having some fun in the cramped apartment.

Sometime after midnight in walked Lindsey, a friend of many
in town. He was wearing a brand-new suit and showed up very
drunk. He had obviously come from another pretty good party,
and his suit looked like he had been sleeping in it for a week.
His eyes had that glazed over look as he headed straight to the
food table. Guy's wife, Karen, always did a fantastic job with the
food!

When he made it to the lunch table, he couldn't resist the three
different types of chicken wings that were waiting for him.
He was grabbing some of each and filling every pocket of his
new wrinkled suit. I thought for sure that the stains from the
honey garlic ones alone would never wash out, but not really my
problem. It was just fun watching him pack away as much food
as he could get. I think he was grocery shopping!

Once he had his pockets full, he headed to the bar and grabbed
himself a drink. He came over to where I was on the couch and
sat his ass down right beside me. He didn't even say hi or grunt
or anything. He was swaying, almost uncontrollably back and
forth. This went on for only couple of minutes, then he looked
up at me and finally talked. "Randy, I'm so damn drunk that
I can't even sit still," and with that he was up off the couch. I
watched in amazement as he made his way to the apartment
door and out he went. We never saw him again that night!

Sometime around 3:00 am, one of the ladies who had left 20
minutes earlier showed up to explain how her boyfriend had
his suburban stuck outside and needed some help. There was
only a few of us left, so we all grabbed our coats and went
outside to see what was going on. When we got there, Lorne
was still behind the steering wheel, and to say he was stuck
was an understatement. His truck was halfway off the road and
in danger of just falling over the cliff some 20 feet down. In
our drunken state, we began going over all the different ways

we could get him out of this mess. There was no damage to anything or anyone, yet!

After talking it over, we all felt that I could just drive my 1 ton 4x4 crew cab right behind his suburban and push him out. With a lot of effort and noise, I managed to get in behind him. I am now on that slope sideways that drops off to nothing good. I managed to push his truck out of that spot. He turned up onto the road as I pushed from behind…mission accomplished! Except, now I was sitting exactly where he had been stuck…I was now stuck!

Lorne drove away with his suburban full of party goers and we were left to get ourselves out. He didn't know we were stuck. Now all that was left was a few of us…Lois, Brian P., Scruff, me and a few others outside. We needed to get my truck out of there before the police showed up. We needed to hurry!

The game plan was a simple one…run my front winch cable way out across the street and wrap it around that one lone power pole. We would use that to winch us out. "Yes, this will work fine," we were thinking. We had no sooner wrapped the cable around that pole when (and I did say at the beginning that "sometimes even the police would show up") and here they were. They drove right over to where my winch cable was tied, and they wanted to know whose smart idea it was to use the power pole as an anchor point. I put my hand up, "Mine," I said. The two officers said, "This is not a good plan at all. If that pole breaks with your winch cable around it, you will be paying for the mess. It will cost you until you're a very old man. Take that cable and attach it to the front of our truck on the steel bars. Then get back inside your truck and winch yourself out of that ditch, before you roll the damn thing."

These two officers never got out of their vehicle as we undid what we had done on the pole and hooked onto to the police cruiser. I overheard one of the officers talking to my wife, who was the soberest one in the group, as slowly we managed to get my truck back up and into the street on level ground. Lois said she was okay to drive, and the officer replied, "Well, just don't let Randy behind the wheel again tonight!" After we had all the cable spooled back onto the winch, I headed over and thanked the nice officers for the extra help. What the hell…they were gone as if they had never been there. Lois drove us all home, and it was a very interesting night to say the least.

We were very lucky to have the officers we did in Inuvik. They helped people in all kinds of ways when they could. I have the utmost respect for the people in uniform, as they did whatever they had to do to keep control of the town. Inuvik was a bit of a transient town. People came, people went, and some of us just stayed!

A rare photo of Zip drunk.

STRANDED IN THE HIGH ARCTIC

This beautiful fall day at our cabin on Ya Ya Lake, which is 90 miles north of Inuvik, couldn't have started out any better. Uncle Dick, Dennis, and I woke up hung over...again! The plan for the day began with us eating some of the best bacon and eggs, that I didn't have to make, while sipping on some coffee and Bailey's, in the hope feeling half human again. This was important as there was another big rye bottle just sitting there waiting for the top to come off and be thrown away.

Once we had finished breakfast, we decided to get our stuff together to head out in Uncle Dick's boat to find us some geese to shoot at. Our travels took us about 40 miles from the cabin up a little creek close to the Arctic Ocean. This is where I should point out our first mistake. We failed to tell anyone where we were going. We had Uncle Dick with us and as long as he was there, we felt safe. He had spent most of his life living up in the arctic, so all was good, or so we thought.

We managed to get the boat a very long way from the main route before we ran out of enough water to go any further. It was time to park the boat and unload our gear, drinks, and some food. We set up our camp and got a nice fire going, and dug out our tarp that we could sit under out of the rain. Did I mention that it was just raining hard enough that the tundra turned to mud, ugly mud!? If you walked in it, your rubber boots would sink into the damn stuff with every step. It made for tough walking. Anybody who has ever had the chance to boat up the mighty Mackenzie River from Inuvik to the Arctic Ocean in the rain will know what kind of mud I am talking about.

As luck would have it, the geese were starting to flock up for their journey south. They were just waiting for the right wind. The geese were too far from us, and we couldn't get to them. The boat was as far as it could go. We couldn't walk through all that mud and muskeg to find a spot where we might get a shot or two. The geese were coming from all directions landing in with the huge flock that was developing about a 1000 yards away from where we were stuck, sitting under our tarp, keeping our drinks dry.

The noise the geese were making was getting louder and louder, so loud in fact, that it was nothing like I had ever heard before. The sound of that many geese in one spot is something that not everybody gets a chance to hear. At times we had to talk very loudly to each other. We sat hoping to get a shot at the odd goose making its way to the growing flock.

We had got to this spot on Thursday night, and had planned to stay until Sunday, then head for home. During our time there, we had only managed to shoot at a couple of very high-flying geese. This resulted in us not having to do all that nasty stuff you have to do with a dead goose…like pluck and clean it, then cook and eat it.

We were using the boat as our bedroom. At least it was dry, as we had a full cover on it. It was hard to pass out properly though, as the cackling was very loud from all the geese that had gathered on that impossible to get to spot. These were snow geese, and I knew how stupid a snow goose is supposed to be. These ones were cunning and smart, and they knew exactly where to sit. They were safe, as long as they stayed right where they were.

On the Saturday night after a long day of sitting around the fire trying to keep warm, and without even one goose, we headed to the boat for some sleep. The noise was deafening. I can't stress enough as to how loud they were! If we weren't so pissed off at noise by now, we just might have figured that we were lucky enough to actually witness how the geese band together before that long trip south. The geese were coming into this big flock all day and night. Every day, there were more and more of them…which made the noise louder and louder. With enough whiskey, beers, and scotch we finally, even with the noise, were able to pass out. What a relief.

Sunday morning came way too quick. The pounding in my head seemed to kick in as I opened one eye, and it got worse after I managed to pry open the other eye. I thought, "Wow, all those geese have given me a huge headache from all their cackling."

It was still drizzling cold rain on us, as it had the whole time we were parked there. We couldn't hear any noise from the geese. It was eerily silent. Not a noise, other than us moving about. The wind had come up a little and the geese had taken advantage of that sometime in the night. Every last one of them was gone. We went from deafening geese chatter to complete calm, no noise at all, but the severe pounding in our heads. I kind of wished the geese were still there. I did not like the noise my own head was making, and I couldn't stop it.

After a few coffees with our main staple, Bailey's (just to add flavour you know), we pulled our big orange tarp down and proceeded to load up the boat to head out. Even though the weather was bad, and we didn't get one goose, we had enjoyed each other's company. We had a lot of laughs, drinks and stories, and fixing the problems of the world, as drinkers do. We had a great time, and I was a little sad to be leaving.

After getting everything into the boat, we settled down in our spots with Uncle Dick at the controls. One turn of the key to start the boat and we knew we were in trouble. The motor didn't even turn over. The key had been left in the auxiliary position and both batteries didn't stand a chance. So, for the entire time we were sit-hunting and drinking as much as possible, the batteries were slowly draining their life away. It had not even occurred to us to check that as we had no need to start the boat while were camped.

As soon as Uncle Dick turned the key and the motor didn't start, he looked back at me and said, "Randy, how much booze we got left?"

I quickly looked through everything that was in the back of the boat and said, "We have one bottle of rye left, (a big bottle I should add), half a bottle of Bailey's, one case of beer, little bit of scotch, and a full bottle of rum".

Uncle then said, without skipping a beat, "Well, let's get the boat unloaded and set up camp again. We may be here awhile." I still wonder, to this day, why Uncle didn't mention food, or how much of that we may have had left...um! Again, I must mention that nobody knew where we were! We had broken a cardinal rule of the North. Always tell somebody where you are going if you head out from town for any reason.

After setting up camp again, Uncle tried the mobile radio we carried in case of emergency, but it happened to work off battery power. Not a plus for us in this situation! As it turned out, the batteries had enough life in them to get through to Aunt Lucille who was at home in Inuvik, about 120 miles from us. Once connected all Uncle Dick could say before the batteries gave out completely was, "We are broken down and need a battery to start the boat. Send a plane with a battery. We are…" and that's when the call ended. We had no way of knowing if anybody would find us. We were way off the beaten path so to speak, out in the middle of no man's land.

Uncle Dick was calm as he said, "Okay looks like we may be here awhile. We need to start rationing the booze we have left." Again, no mention of food!

Much later in the day we could hear a plane flying and we spotted it. It was just a small dot in the sky a very long way away from us. We spread out our big, bright orange tarp on the mud, and we got a nice big fire going with lots of smoke so that the plane could find us. This was Sunday, as I mentioned earlier, and the plane was flying a grid pattern that was taking him further away from us. That broke our spirits a little. Now, we really had to slow down on the liquor consumption.

Night arrived and we were back in the boat trying hard to sleep. Passing out was out of the question, because of the ration ban on the booze. The next morning, we were up early and watching the empty sky for a plane. Finally, again we could hear the engine of the plane, but very faintly. This time he was looking way off in a different area again. Shit. We were disappointed. We knew we had to try another day of rationing the damn booze!

Well, Monday slowly, very slowly, turned into night and we still had no hope of being found. Back to the boat for another restless night of rolling around and trying to get comfortable enough to sleep. It was sobering to know we were running out of supplies and no one was looking in our area. It was also affecting my passing out, that I was used to.

Tuesday morning came and we started our day much the same as Monday. We got out of the boat to just sit and wait, and finally we talked about our food shortage. With no geese on hand, and no fish where we were, we decided to go look for some ptarmigan to shoot. We quickly abandoned that idea, as the muskeg and mud were way too hard to walk in. Back to camp we went to do some more waiting.

Finally, again, we could hear the drone of the plane engine and our spirits went up a notch. This time it sounded closer…and yes, soon we could see it. The three of us quickly grabbed the big bright orange tarp and started waving it, and yes, we even started to yell. I'm not sure why we were yelling at the plane. I am guessing that we only did it out of desperation. Our rationed booze was pretty much gone by now, and food was getting to be scarce as well.

It looked like the plane was doing a grid pattern that would bring it closer and closer to us…so more smoke from the fire and more tarp waving and more yelling kept us busy, as we watched the plane turn in the opposite direction once again! Another restless night spent in the boat.

Wednesday morning came and so did the worrying that we had not talked about until today. Trying to stay positive was getting just a bit harder for all three of us by now. Uncle Dick was doing his best to reassure Dennis and myself that somebody will find us sooner than later. Uncle was tough as a rock in many ways, and he wasn't going to let this bother him. No matter what, he was always the strong one when it came right down to it.

Around noon we again heard the plane that had been looking for us. Back to tarp waving and yes, yelling as well. I will say that I think we were even yelling louder as the plane sounded closer. I guess we thought if we yelled really loud the pilot would be able to hear us over the noise of the engine. The plane was close, but we could tell from where we were that he still hadn't seen us.

With only one flare to shoot up we took this opportunity to use it. Uncle Dick fired it up in the air while Dennis and I continued to wave and yell. Then the plane turned towards us and did the wave thing with his wings. Yay, all our yelling paid off! He had seen us, but he had no way to get to us. Remember, we were a long way off the main water channel, and he couldn't land close to us.

The pilot put his float plane down on the water at least a mile from us. We started the hard walk to where he was, all the while helping each other. When one of us would get stuck in the mud, the other two would try to pull you out, without losing a rubber boot to the mud. It was very hard to do and very tiring! Once we finally made it to the plane, there were hugs all the way around.

The pilot reaches into the plane and grabs a case of beer and hands it to Uncle Dick and says, "Thought you guys might be needing some of these by now." Boy, did he brighten up three tired, hungry, thirsty, and stinky guys' day with a simple case of beer.

Rescue plane

After chatting with the pilot for a bit while we guzzled down a couple of beers, Uncle Dick asked him if by chance, he brought a battery or two with him for the boat. Much to our excitement he had…but our excitement quickly fizzled. Now, we must pack two batteries all the way back through the mud and muskeg to where the boat was. It was, I thought, a hard walk to the plane while carrying nothing.

The weight of the batteries sure added to the problem. We kept having to leapfrog the batteries to each other, as well as pull ourselves though the mud and muskeg. It was the longest and hardest walk I have ever had to do.

Once we were back at the boat and the new batteries installed, the motor fired right up. We could say good riddance to our little place we had called home for more days than we originally had intended.

Looking back on that now, I am feeling somewhat happy that the key was left on in the boat. I got to spend some quality time with one of my most favourite people in this world, a very special person to a lot of people, my Uncle Dick!

The boat we slept in while waiting to be rescued. Finally, we're heading home.

MONEY TREE
AT THE MACKENZIE

Damad Productions and Consulting was a company that Brian P., Guy, and I started to help bring patrons into the Mackenzie Hotel for Walter. Basically, we made up contests, talent shows, and other forms of entertainment to draw people to the bar.

Damad Productions was making plans that would hopefully fill the bar up to capacity and beyond in December. Normally it was hard to get big crowds in the Christmas month, because of staff parties all over town. Over the few months that we had been planning ways to bring in big crowds, we had done exactly that, except nothing ever seemed to go according to plan. We had tried a few different ways to help the bar, but this time we had a winner...or so we thought!

Guy, Brian P., and I had tossed around a few ideas to get this bar hopping full, and we came up with our best idea yet. We needed Walter, the owner, to donate $100 in one dollar bills. We would go get a Christmas tree and with wooden clothes pins attach all those bills onto the tree.

Walter even liked the idea, so the Saturday before the event we set out to go find a good tree somewhere down the Dempster highway. Walter paid for our gas and threw in some whiskey, so that we wouldn't die from thirst in our quest to find the perfect tree. It took most of the day to find "the one", but find it we did. What luck! We had just enough booze left to get us home… thank you, Walter!

Back in town we had a few things to do. First, we needed to make some posters, even the primitive posters we made, then we drove around and stuck them up all over town. We knew the guys at the radio station, so we let them know about our endeavour. They offered up some free airtime for the week leading into the next Saturday.

Things were really starting to come together. We had tickets to sell at the front door, which allowed you in for the night, and your name in the barrel to win. You see, the name pulled out would have exactly 15 seconds to grab as many bills off that tree as possible from right in the middle of the dance floor.

Saturday arrived, just like always, except this day was going to have an awesome night in the Mackenzie bar. All plans were finished, and now we just had to get through the day so that we could begin setting up our new and improved "Damad Game of Chance". All our work seemed to be paying off. By 8:00 pm the bar was near full. We were not pulling the name out of the barrel until 11:00 pm.

We were shocked at how fast the bar was filling up. Walter, on the other hand, just had a huge grin on his face as the bartender was barely keeping up with the waitress' orders.

The three of us decided that we should set the tree up at about 10:00 pm to get the crowd excited! As soon as we entered the bar carrying this tree full of money, the bar was going wild with excitement, but then again, they were all mostly drunk by now…an easy audience to have fun with. This change of plans, bringing the tree out earlier than right at 11:00 pm, was working awesome. There were lots of loud drinkers, and they were getting louder as the time was getting closer to the money hour of 11 o'clock.

The time was up. It was time to get up in front of the crowd and pull that name out to see who was going to have a chance at some free dollars. As we were stretching this out with talk and name mixing…remember back at the beginning of this story when I wrote that "we had a winner… or so we thought"… well, right then, the back door of the pub opened and coming through it at a dead run heading straight to that tree was some dude I didn't know. We all watched in shock as he grabbed up the tree, turned and ran completely out the door he just came through. This all took maybe 10 seconds or less.

The three of us were looking at each other and it took a moment for all that to sink in. Then, off we ran to try and catch this tree thief. We found the tree on the ground about a half a block away. He was nowhere to be seen, and our tree was missing almost all the money, but he did not get it all! Holy jumping bullfrogs was that guy ever fast on his feet carrying a big old tree.

We ended up getting more money from Walter to put back on what was now a sad and battered looking tree, missing some branches, but at least this time it went better.

TINY DROPS OF WATER

Every winter we couldn't wait for summer so that we could boat up the Mackenzie River to spend time at Uncle Dick's cabin. Now don't get me wrong here, we loved some parts of the winter as well. Karate class on Monday evenings was fun. The men's and ladies' dart leagues at the Legion on Tuesday evenings, as well as shuffle board and pool were fun on any night. We also filled up Wednesday evenings with some fast-paced basketball games in the school gym. That was also fun. Thursdays was usually reserved for just hanging out at the Legion and bull shitting with the guys and gals around the bar, tended by a wonderful lady named Del… that was a great time. With curling Friday evenings and some bonspiels on weekends with our buddies, who were all competitive, winter kept us busy and amused.

As summer approached, all our winter schedules would slowly change to our summer schedules, and the most important item on our new schedule, year in and year out, was to get the boat ready and any problems fixed. We always hoped for a bunch of weekends filled with boating up to Ya Ya lakes, to Uncle's cabin. Some of these trips didn't go as planned. This story is about anti-social distancing. In other words, those weekends where the cabin beds were filled to capacity.

We usually had about 12-14 people sleeping in close quarters. These were the weekends filled with the most fun, as there was always something going on: shooting skeet, drinking, playing cards, drinking, fishing, drinking, hunting, drinking. You see, there were lots of things to fill our weekends up with.

The only problem was if you were needing some "alone" time with your girlfriend, or new wife, it was tough to find a spot to get that out of your system. The best and possibly only spot was out in the middle of the lake in the boat. You could put the seats down so you could actually lay down. Nobody could see us, not even with binoculars. Now that's another story by itself.

Lois and I decided we needed some "alone" time out in the boat. Away we went, out to the middle, far from everyone. We would certainly hear any boats approaching. Of course, we had our baby, Scott, with us. It was also tough to get him to nap in the afternoon, in the noisy cabin. Scott always fell asleep a few minutes into a boat ride. Off we went.

The lake was very calm this day, a beautiful summer day to be out on the water and get some sun on our bodies. Clothes were shed within a few minutes after shutting the motor off. It was "alone" time, finally!

We were laying down on those cushioned seats after our so called "alone" time was over and done, without those pesky clothes. We were just enjoying the sun, peace, and quiet of the world around us. We could hear a slight noise coming from the cabin far off. We had drifted closer during our fun, but that was about it. We were so comfy, and with Scotty fast asleep, we also drifted off to some much needed sleep!

Then, came a sound; the sound that woke us both up. Almost like some droplets of water hitting the lake, small drops, but nonetheless they sounded close by. I quickly lifted my head and peered over the side of the boat. Right there, within 10 feet of us, was my cousin in one of the small fishing boats holding a boat oar in his hands. When our eyes met, he was still holding the water dripping oar in his hands, not moving a muscle. This moment in time, right now, got real awkward. Not a word was spoken for what seemed like minutes, maybe seconds was the real time. With Lois not being able to get up quite yet, due to a clothes finding problem, I blurted out to my cousin, "Hey, what the hell you doing way out here!"

Our "alone time" boat, now with cover!

Of course, he lied when he said he thought we maybe broke down and needed some help. I replied with, "Well, why didn't you just drive on over with the kicker motor on the back?"

His reply was, "I thought I would save some gas!"

"Save gas, my ass. You were sneaking up on us just to catch us making out." Lucky for us, he wasn't that sneaky. That droplet of water, when we were sleeping naked in a floating boat, sounded like a bomb going off.

After almost getting caught way out in the middle of the lake like that, we were much more creative on picking just the right spot for our "alone" time!

Left to right: Yvonne (Randy's mom), Uncle Dick, and Aunty Lucille on the deck of the cabin.

NO FIGHTING ALLOWED

I was only involved in two altercations inside the Legion walls. This is one of the stories.

Let me say first off, fighting in the Legion was a big no-no, and would usually get you banned for up to 6 months or more, or kicked out for good. Either way, if you did fight, you had to go up in front of the main board members, in a closed door meeting, to explain your side and see what punishment they would vote on.

My first incident in the Legion happened when I first moved to Inuvik in the mid 1970s. I did not go in there looking or wanting to fight anyone. I was in there because I loved to drink whiskey with a bunch of people around the bar. I was in there for the fun, not to fight.

On this day, the Legion was pretty busy. The stand-up bar where the regular, die-hard customers had claimed their spot to stand was full. This was where the fun was.

I had only been in Inuvik a short time, so I had the rookie's spot at the far end, while my Uncle Dick would stand at his spot on the exact opposite side. In-between us there were usually 7-10 guys or gals in their respective spots. Now, if a regular was not in the building, you could stand in their spot. Should that person show up, you would get the old stink eye look until you gathered up your things and moved to your own spot.

Today was Saturday and everyone was having some fun as usual, while Del, the lady behind the bar, was in her usual joyful mood and making us laugh while she kept busy. She could get a bunch of things done and still have time for us drinkers. She was our superwoman who not only kept the drinks coming, but was also quick with the wit. It was tough to get anything over on her. We all loved her, and we listened to her and we respected her in every way!

I was standing in my usual spot at the bar when this fella walks in and stands in the only empty place left, which just happened to be right beside me. I didn't know this guy at all, maybe because I had only been in Inuvik for a few months. I noticed he ordered a whiskey and coke, same as I drank, so I'm thinking to myself he must be a good guy. I know, I have a low bar in choosing friends. If you drink whiskey, you're my friend, period! I also noticed that this guy looked rather tough. He was about three inches shorter than me and he was packing some pretty big arms to go with those wide shoulders. Not the type of guy that a young 21-year-old weighing in at a solid 135 pounds would want to wrestle with. That alone would also make him my friend.

The spot that we were standing in at the bar was right across from the back door leading in and out of the building. The front door was used way more often since the parking lot was right out that door.

After having a few laughs and drinks with the crowd around the bar, something went terribly wrong, and to this day I'm not quite sure who got mad at who first. But the tensions were running high and now the two of us were arguing over something, neither of us backing down. He didn't back down, because he must have known he was tough. I, on the other hand, didn't back down, because I had been drinking whiskey a lot longer that day than this guy, and thought I was tough.

Del could see this was escalating rather quickly and the rules are the rules…no fighting in the Legion. Finally, she had enough of me and new guy yelling at each other. She yelled, "Hey, you two, no fighting in here! Get outside if you want to fight".

The two of us looked at each other, and yeah we were both mad as hell. New guy says, "Wanna go out back and finish this out there?"

"Sure," I answered. "Let's go!"

By now we had everyone's attention as we both hurried to the back door. He hurried faster than I did and got through the door to the outside with me right behind him. When I got to the door, I slammed it shut and locked it. Then, I calmly walked back to my drink at the bar. New guy was banging on the locked door and yelling at me to get out there and quit being a chicken (and other crap).

I didn't pay any attention to that noise which we all could hear quite plainly through the back door. By now the guys around the bar were starting to laugh. They thought that was pretty cool of me letting him go first then locking him out, and I was quite proud of thinking that fast. Hell, I didn't want to fight this guy…even he knew he was tough!

While all were listening and laughing at what just took place, the noise outside that door quit. I never gave it another thought as we figured he finally went home. As it turned out, not many of the guys around the bar knew the fella either, other than seeing him every once in a while inside the Legion.

After the noise quit at the back door, it took about one minute to see the one major flaw of my well thought out plan…and that flaw was coming through the front door of the Legion at a fast pace towards me yelling at me!

"What's the matter, chicken shit? You forgot to lock the front door? Now what are you going to do?" The laughter stopped for just a brief moment. In that time he was getting close to me. The laughter started again, only much louder and pointed in my direction this time.

"Oh shit," I thought, "I'm going to have to fight this big scary guy and get beat up bad." He was red-faced mad when he finally reached me at the bar.

He was pretty loud when he asked me what the hell I locked the door on him for. I replied with something like, "Well buddy, I'm not stupid. Look at you, then look at me…who do you think was going to get hurt? There was no way I was going to go outside with you!" He stared at me all huffed up like a mad dog for a minute or so, while the guys watching were trying hard not to laugh…much!

That moment, that exact moment, seemed like forever for me. I was expecting a punch heading my way and wondering how I was going to fight back. As he continued his stare at me, I stared back. I needed to keep my eyes on him so that I could have time to at least duck out of the way before I got what I deserved.

After that long stare down, he spoke first.

He says in a much calmer voice now, "That was pretty smart of you to lock that door... must have been funny from this side, eh?"

I couldn't lie to this guy. I said, "Yeah, we thought it was funny. We were all kind of laughing at you until you came through the front door mad as hell, and yelling at me. Then everyone started laughing at me instead. It was then that I knew I was in trouble!"

With that last remark he looks at my empty glass on the bar in front of me and says, "What're you drinking?"

"Whiskey and coke," I replied.

He looks at Del and says, "Two whiskeys, please. One for this guy and one for me." This surprised everyone within listening distance. I thanked him as I stuck my hand out and said, "My name's Randy." He takes my hand and shakes it and says, "My name's Dallas."

We became very good friends after that and spent many days drinking together...as it turns out, he was a great guy for a new guy!

I liked this guy a lot. He was funny and liked whiskey. He was tough and he was now my friend. He was a good enough human being that I stole his name and called my first son... Dallas!

CUSTOMER SATISFACTION IN INUVIK

My job at the industrial store in Inuvik was not so much a job, but a place to go see my friends and have some fun while doing some work! It was awesome. We had a ton of laughs together and really enjoyed all the fun shit that could happen at any moment. It was a prankster's paradise. Even if you were hungover, you still had to watch your back and be prepared for whatever your friends and co-workers may have in store for you.

Today we were all going to learn something; we just didn't know it quite yet. A few weeks back, Peter, one of the welders in town, had been in to buy some new oxygen and acetylene gauges. A fairly simple request, we only carried two different types in stock...the cheaper version that would be perfect for the home guy on his set of bottles, or the more expensive ones that a guy like Peter, who works everyday with these, should be using.

First, let me give you a little background on Peter. He was just one of many welders in town running a business and trying to stay afloat and times were not always rosy for welders in Inuvik. In all the years I dealt with him, I had ever met a guy quite like him. He didn't remind me of anybody; he didn't act like anybody. He was, let's say, just different than the rest of the crowd!

He took pride in saying that when all his bills came due at the end of the month, he would put all the names on pieces of paper and toss them all in a hat. He would pull three names out, and those were the three companies that he would pay that month. Sometimes, it would be three or four months before our name came out of that hat. He would walk into our store and announce that we were the lucky ones who won "the Peter's lottery", and he would bring us a cheque. Peter was a weird fella in that regard, but all in all, you just couldn't help but like him. He was harmless and even funny sometimes.

Peter brought back the set of cheaper gauges that we had sold him a few short weeks earlier. They had just quit working for whatever reason. He was kind of pissy about it. He was telling us that having to come back to the store was costing him money and that he wanted, not only a complete refund or a new set of gauges, but also to charge us for his time.

Seeing as Guy was our manager, he got to deal with shit like this. After a slight little argument between the two, Peter ended up leaving the store with a brand-new set of free gauges…the cheaper ones again!

A week later, maybe even less, as I think about it, Peter comes strolling into the store. Right up to the front counter all smiles for a change. I was thinking maybe we won the lottery and he was paying off his long overdue account with us. Guy was thinking the same thing, so he went up to the counter to see what Peter needed, in hopes of a cheque coming his way.

Peter asks Guy, "Can I get a 10lb sledge hammer, please." Guy goes out to the warehouse and brings one up to the counter for him.

"Is that everything today, Peter," Guy asked as he started pulling out an invoice to write up the sale.

At this point Peter said, "No. No, I don't want to buy it. I just need it for a moment."

Peter now had everybody's attention. He grabbed the sledge hammer and started heading back out the door to the outside. We all were just left standing with these perplexed looks on our faces, wondering what the hell he was up to.

As soon as Peter's hand touched the door to leave, he turned to see us all just standing there, as if waiting for a cab or something. He says out loud, "You guys want to see some customer satisfaction? Follow me."

Guy and Wayne, with me not far behind, start heading to the front door to see what this was all about. We didn't want to miss a minute. Once outside the building, we see, on the cement door step, the set of gauges Guy had given him not too long before. Peter had all of our attention as he swung that 10lb sledge hammer into the gauges, over and over, until they were just a bunch of broken pieces laying everywhere. We watched his little display without a word.

When he was done, he said, "That's what customer satisfaction looks like. Don't ever sell me these crap gauges again." And with

80

that he put the sledge hammer against the outside wall, looked Guy straight in the eyes and said, "I'm returning the hammer as I no longer need it."

Once Peter was out of the parking lot, the bunch of us couldn't stop laughing. We had told Peter twice that he needed the more expensive gauges, as the cheaper ones were actually made for the hobby guy, not for the professional guy who uses them every day for work.

That was a good day. A customer kept us talking and laughing for a very long time. Guy said it was all worth it, "Customer satisfaction." Ha! Ha! Ha!

WINTER DRIVE TO AKLAVIK WITH FRIENDS

When a good friend asks if you want to go for a drive to Aklavik, or anywhere for that matter, on the ice road, you usually go for safety reasons. Especially if this friend is buying the booze for the trip.

My good friend Brian P. had to go to Aklavik to look at a painting job that he was going to bid on. It was a very cold Saturday, and I didn't much feel like giving up my spot at the bar in the Legion. But again, safety first in the North, with booze coming in a close second. We were 2 for 2 on that, so I guess we were heading to Aklavik to check out this job.

Brian P. decided that we should have a couple of drinks while we were talking about the trip and about how much booze we needed to get us there and back. During our discussion, in walked Guy, my boss from work. After hearing what we were planning for the day, he wanted in on that drive. Sometimes it was just nice to get out of town, even if it was only for the company.

The truck of choice in Inuvik was mostly single cabs with 4 wheel drive. Brian P.'s truck was a single cab, but only the two wheel drive variety. This was not usually the truck you wanted for ice road travel, especially for as far as we had to go. I think it was normally an hour or hour and half drive one way. I'm not exactly sure as I think booze clouded my distance reading ability as well as really throwing off my time clock. It didn't bother me much as long as fun was involved, and believe me, going anywhere with these two friends of mine, fun was going to happen!

Time was starting to slip away and with little to no sunlight this time of year, it was usually best to travel in the middle of the day. We really needed to get out of the Legion soon, but Brian P. was buying, so Guy and I were in no hurry to leave this place quite yet.

After a few more drinks in our bellies, it was time to get on that ice and drive. But first we stopped at the town's liquor store so that Brian P. could pick up our promised booze for the drive over. Brian P. picked up a 40oz of rum for himself, and two 40oz bottles of rye, one for me and one for Guy. A quick stop at the corner store to pick up some much-needed coke to mix with our drinks, and we were headed towards the boat launch where the ice road started.

Brian P. was driving. I had the middle seat and that put Guy by the passenger door. It was a tight fit as we needed winter clothes, big warm boots, and the alcohol and mix were taking up some leg room as well. The drive over was a bunch of laughs as we didn't have a care in the world other than get to our destination and back home… safely!

We made it over to Aklavik as planned. We were three pretty happy guys, slightly drunk happy guys I guess would describe us better at this point.

When you went on road trips to other communities, it was tough to get away once you were in town. You see, the local people enjoyed seeing company come to town, and these communities were so small everyone knew you were there half an hour before you were actually there. So we spent a bit of time in town talking with whomever wanted conversation, learning some things from the local town folk. They were all very friendly and listening to them tell stories could keep a fella's interest for hours. We didn't have that kind of time, so we stayed for a bit, then went back to the truck for the trip home, much drunker than when we had left some hours previously.

The seating arrangements inside the truck were the same as the drive over. We were having a blast enjoying our time together, while sipping a few ice road pops to bring out the best in all of us, or the worst, depending on your point of view. Sitting in between these two lifelong friends of mine was just perfect for me. I enjoyed the crazy of both these guys and we were usually all on the same page in the humour department. I'm pretty sure a lot of you have had these kinds of trips with your good drinking buddies. You can well imagine the fun shit that was being thrown around inside that crowded cab.

At this point in the trip, which was about half way back to Inuvik, I noticed that the booze had overtaken the number one spot – safety. It was quite clear that safety became number two as the booze was flowing from bottle to cup faster than on the trip over to Aklavik. Usually something happens when those two switch positions, and that something was usually bad. Once in a blue moon it could be good, but tonight there was no "blue moon" out at all.

With darkness for the trip home, it was proving to be a bit tougher of a drive. I can only describe it as being "inside a cow's belly" dark! Now maybe, just maybe, the booze might have been impairing our judgment, but the three of us did not think that was the case here. It was a good thing that the ice road was ploughed pretty wide. Apparently, we needed all that room as Brian P.'s ability to drive straight was quickly diminishing. Guy and I barely even noticed. Being drunk is not performance enhancing at all, so don't let anyone tell you any different. Trust me!

We did not see this coming. There was no warning. One minute it was fun and calm, the next minute turmoil, as we found ourselves spinning totally out of control in the middle of the ice road. Brian P. threw his full drink on the floor so that he could use both hands on the wheel. I'm not sure why he did that; we had no control at all. We were just three guys, like on a bad ride at a county fair, that couldn't be stopped. Brian P. was trying to get us under control. Meanwhile, Guy was hitting his head on the passenger window and then my shoulder, again and again, spilling his full drink all over the cab. I was lucky to be in the middle, or maybe I was smart, as the other two were keeping me from moving much. I was wedged in to start with. I didn't spill a single drop of my drink.

The spinning around and around didn't stop until we ended up hitting the high snow bank on the edge of the road. We hit it so hard that everything inside the cab changed position. There was a moment of silence after we hit the snow bank. I'm not sure if it was a moment of silence for the lost drinks, or if we were trying to just figure out what happened so damn quickly.

We kind of took stock of each other and both Brian P. and Guy pointed out that I hadn't spilled my drink at all, while both theirs were in puddles on the floor.

All three of us got out to survey our problem, and we were surprised to see how stuck we were. The truck was facing exactly backwards of the direction we had been driving in. It was so frigging dark out that we really were having trouble seeing much. Brian P. gets this drunk idea to launch a distress flair up into the air so that we could see better. Oh, oh…this was going to be our "something happens" moment when booze takes the number one position over safety. As soon as that flair lit up the dark night as if it was daylight, we saw two things. One thing was the damn near buried truck backwards in the snow bank and the second thing was the big fuel tanks right on outskirts of Inuvik. It was exactly then we realized all of Inuvik would have seen that flair, just as clear as we could.

I am not quite sure if I have ever witnessed three guys moving so fast, as we knew the police would be on their way soon to see who needed help. The rule with flairs was <u>only</u> use them if you're in a bad spot of trouble. Well, we were, but drunk was not going to help when the police showed up! Brian P. grabbed a shovel out of the back of the truck and immediately went to work on getting his truck out of the mess he had put it in. Guy and I were helping with empty five-gallon buckets to move the snow. I can't stress enough how quick we were moving, as we figured we had five minutes at best before the police would be taking us away. Brian P. was like a little Tasmanian devil, fast and efficient in his shovelling. We needed to get out of here before trouble showed up to take us in.

We figured it was time for Brian P. to get back behind the wheel. Guy and I pushed and with Brian P. driving, we managed to get the old girl rocking back and forth, back and forth. With us working together, shit, we somehow managed to get the truck back onto the ice road and turned towards Inuvik. There was still no police lights coming yet. The three of us piled back into the truck and took off towards town, and possible trouble. There was only this road, but it did have two different spots you could leave town to get on this ice road... one was on this end of town and the other on the other end. We elected to try and make it past Inuvik to the second road, as we thought the police would be using the first ramp in and out of town towards where the flair went up.

To this day, I do not know how we got out of that situation.

As soon as we made it up on the farthest ramp, we could see the lights of the police and rescue trucks going down the ramp we had just driven by... really fast. They were headed to where we had just been. We did what we thought wouldn't attract any attention to us. We went to the Legion for a few drinks! Eventually, I'm sure we told everyone in that building what happened to us.

Our lesson here was again...Safety first, booze second. Did we always do that in the proper order? Hell, no!

FISHING OFF PONTOONS

What a small world we live in. I was bored and decided to go driving down the Dempster highway, the one and only road that connects Inuvik with the rest of the world. Every year, more and more tourists were coming up to poke around, buy some souvenirs, and take in the Northern culture. Many of these tourists were mildly surprised by how things were up north. Everybody had the same thing to say about the local elders, or just people in general, in this small town; and it was not uncommon to hear tourists talk about how friendly everyone was to them.

It was a beautiful day in Inuvik. Spring had already sprung for us, and I was just happy the sun was shining again, all day and into the night. I jumped into the truck and decided a Dempster drive would be perfect on this Saturday, while waiting for the Legion to open. I was about a half hour out of town when a vehicle went by heading towards Inuvik.

"I remember that international truck," I thought to myself. I was sure that was Gene's vehicle. He was a good friend of my dad's, and we had on occasion hunted together when I lived down south. Every year, Gene would come out to Brandon, Manitoba to hunt deer with us, so I was pretty sure that was Gene just heading the other way. I only drove on about a mile when I thought, "Hell, why would Gene be coming to Inuvik? Certainly not to visit me." As a matter of fact, I wasn't even sure he knew I lived up here. I wasn't even sure that it was Gene; it all happened so fast. I didn't get a good look at the driver.

I couldn't take it any longer. I had to turn around and head back to town to find that vehicle that I thought was Gene's.

Once back in town I started doing what I call a grid search of the streets, looking for the truck, and hopefully it was Gene's. I went up one street and down another. I must say that trying to do a grid search in the maze of streets that were built in town was, at the very least, really hard to do! Some were dead end streets; some were cul du sacs. I ended up doing the random street search instead.

This way worked out way better as I spotted that truck parked in front of a trailer in town. The trailer, and a few others beside it, were home for some of the pilots that would come up to work for the local small airline companies. These guys were known as the bush pilots. In the summer season, they flew pontoon planes, mostly delivering goods all over our region to places like Aklavik, Tuk, and many camps along the Mackenzie River, and even some more isolated camps on landlocked lakes.

I shut the truck off in front of this trailer and jumped out. I went and knocked on the door. A fella I didn't know answered. I know he must have thought I was kind of crazy when I asked him if there was a guy inside named Gene. I got a funny look, but he said, "Yeah, why?" It was about this time that out from the living room comes Gene to see who is at the door.

Gene is my dad's good friend, as well as my hunting partner and friend. Even though he was my dad's age, we got along great on many hunting trips together. Now people usually don't just show up in Inuvik all by themselves. They don't just go out for a drive and end up in Inuvik. Gene lived in British Colombia, which was a very long way from this trailer he was standing in. What was he doing here?

It turned out that Gene did know I lived in Inuvik, and the guy living in that trailer, Craig, was also good friends with my old hunting partner. My life in Inuvik was going to have a bunch of fun added to it. I just didn't know that part yet.

Gene managed to stay in town flying with Craig whenever it was allowed, as there were some strict rules flying these company planes. If a pilot was heading out to deliver goods or people, and coming back with people from wherever they flew to, then they couldn't take a ride along person with them. But if they went anywhere in a plane and was coming back to town empty, the pilots could take someone for company and safety reasons for the flight back home. This, as it turned out, was going to be great for me.

I ended up visiting with Gene and his friend Craig every single day that I could. It was fun telling stories about each other while having a few drinks, reminiscing on the old days gone by, and getting to know Craig as well. But then a fella like Gene couldn't stay forever. So, the day came when Gene left to head back down the highway to home again. After that, Craig and I became good friends. We were about the same age and had a lot in common. Plus, I liked that he flew planes for a living!

One Saturday morning, I was woken up from a deep passed-out

sleep. That damn phone was ringing way too early for my liking. I answered and it was Craig. He said he was heading out to a remote bush camp to drop some goods off for some people out there, and coming home empty. I woke up real quick when I heard the words, "I'm coming home empty and wondered if you want to come along for the flight."

Well, yes I did. "What time?" I asked.

"Right now," he said. "Can you get here in ten minutes?"

I answered with a quick yes. I hopped into my clothes and off I went to the runway in town. I always had a passion for planes, just never tried to get that licence. I drank a lot back then and flying drunk was not going to end well for me.

We delivered the goods, which made the people in that camp happy. It was tough living out there, but the landscape was dotted with such camps, many like my Uncle Dick's cabin at Ya Ya Lakes.

Back up into the air we went. Craig had some time to fly me around sightseeing. He was in no rush to get back today, so off we went to explore. Seeing things from up in the air was interesting and fun enough that I didn't even notice I wasn't hung over anymore.

Craig was a great guide, explaining things that I didn't know about, showing me some beautiful scenery with landlocked bodies of water everywhere you looked. The whole delta area from up there looked like a maze of waterways, and I could see why people got lost if they didn't pay attention down there on the water. I was really enjoying the ride and the company, and I had a nice little smile on my face as we flew wherever Craig felt like.

Off in the distance in front of us was a fairly big lake. We seemed to be heading towards it. We were slowly getting lower and lower, when Craig says, "Why don't we land down there and have a look, and take a bit of a break?"

I was totally good with that, so down we went and he landed the float plane on the clear lake. The water was calm, not a ripple on it until we got there. Craig jumped out of his seat and got on the pontoon. I don't know why, but I did the same. We stood for a moment taking in all that fresh air, the quietness… it was just a very peaceful moment. Here I was in the middle of nowhere and on a very beautiful lake…heaven would look like this to a fisherman!

Craig went back into the plane for a moment while I was taking in the beauty of our surroundings. He comes out with two fishing rods. "Wanna fish?" he says. "Of course, I do!" was my response.

There I was, standing on the back of one pontoon, with Craig right across from me on the other pontoon, casting for fish, any fish. I didn't even know what fish lived here. The casting was not going well for catching anything, so after maybe 10 minutes he asked me if I wanted to try trolling. I was perplexed by that. How in the hell can you troll for fish with a plane? Of course, I said yes anyway. He jumped back into the plane, fired it up and as near as I can figure, he put it into first gear and pointed the nose towards the other side of the lake. He then came back to his pontoon, and we both let some line out. Slowly the plane was headed to the far shore. It was just a matter of minutes when he caught the first of the many trout we would catch that day.

I was so happy I had a new friend; I was so happy that I was fishing where only a plane could take me; I was so happy that

I just fished and grinned. Craig took me on a few different adventures in that plane. I was really liking my new friend.

Without meeting Gene on the highway that day, I may have missed this story you are reading, along with some other great adventures with Craig. I'm glad I went for that drive down the Dempster Highway.

OFF TO TUK TO PICK UP STUFF

We woke up to a beautiful spring day in Inuvik. The sun was shining. The winter ice road was near its melt, meaning that the river would soon be filled with people in boats going out to their remote camps to fish, hunt, drink, and just have some out of town time. This was the time of year that we all waited for. Those long winter days and nights were behind us, and it was starting out to be a pretty good Saturday for us northern folk.

Lois and I went down to the Legion right after lunch to go see what everyone was up to. Inside it was buzzing with talk of the coming summer and plans were being made, even though all that could change in a hurry. Plans were really never set in stone, which was just the way of life in the north.

Cousin Harry came through the door and headed over to us. We had a few drinks, played some darts, had a few laughs, and talked about the upcoming trips to Uncle's cabin that we were all looking forward to. I'm not sure why, on such a nice day, that we left our homes to go enjoy some of that fresh spring air, and then drive to the Legion, park the truck and go inside that building... go figure!

We were having a bit of fun as the day progressed, and it looked like we were settling in for another marathon drinking session. I guess that was normal for us. But like I said, plans can change in a hurry, and one phone call changed our plans instantly. That call came from one of our friends up in Tuk.

He phoned the Legion as he knew us too well. He figured that's where we would be. He told us he had the items ready that Uncle Dick needed for the cabin, and if we still needed them, then we better get up there today as the ice road maintenance crew were going to shut the road down due to severe melting. We said, "Yes, we will be there." If we didn't get the stuff now, we would have to wait until the following winter. The things he had for us were all pretty heavy items and hauling them by boat would not work well in our small boats. We needed to go get them, and bring them back to Inuvik. We left the Legion rather fast. We grabbed some whiskey and rum from the liquor store, then hit the gas station to fill up my 1 ton crew cab 4x4 truck. Then, off onto the ice road the three of us went.

We were all smiles as this was going to be a good trip. We were outside in the sun; we were getting the things Uncle needed, plus we never had to stop our day drinking to do it. The sun was up and the days were long, so time didn't mean anything. But the ice road would prove to mean everything.

As we were making good time on the ice, we did notice that along the way there looked to be a few trouble spots. Water on top of the ice, for instance, could be a big problem, as you couldn't tell what was under that water. When we got to Bar C,

95

which was the turn that goes towards Tuk, there was water everywhere and driving through it slow was the only way to get through the spot. We noted right then that we had better quit dragging our asses, get to Tuk, and hurry back before this got worse. I will also say at this point we had not seen another vehicle at all on the road, which was another red flag we had ignored. We were getting slightly worried about our timing now, and wondered if we should we turn around and go back, or just carry on the last 30 miles, getting there and back as quickly as possible. We chose to continue on.

We pulled into Tuk and went straight to our buddy's place. Without much talk, we loaded up the back of the truck. Shit, I didn't think we were getting this much stuff. We had to load it just right to fit it all, which took a bit of time… time we didn't really have!

As we finished loading everything that we went for, our friend said to get our asses back to Inuvik and be careful on the ice road. It was getting worse by the minute. Fuck, it was a 2 hour drive back to Inuvik at the best of times. This was not the best of times for sure.

The sun was high in the sky as we left to head back and it didn't take long to see how much the road had deteriorated in just the last hour.

We made it back to Bar C, which was the very worst area, and there was finally another vehicle up ahead, but it was stopped. When we pulled up to the vehicle, we saw he was one of the road maintenance guys. He was putting up signs that read "Road Closed" with red ribbons everywhere. Also, the water was visible for a very long ways compared to when we went through a mere two hours earlier. He waved us to a stop and asked where we thought we were going. I replied, "Inuvik."

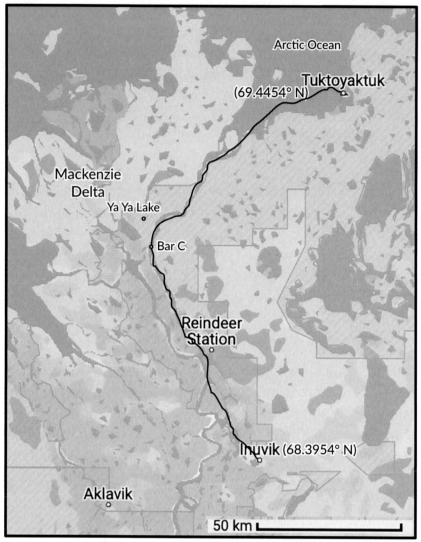

Approximate route of the Mackenzie Ice Road from Inuvik to Tuktoyaktuk.

"No way are you going to Inuvik today with that truck. Just look around," he warned us. Up ahead we could see geysers of water shooting up from the ice to at least 15 feet in the air. They were everywhere. Plus, there was water laying on the ice for as far as we could see ahead of us and on either side of us. I told the guy we needed to get this load back to Inuvik. He told us, "No way,

97

you won't make it. The road is done for the year." He wanted us to drive back to Tuk, leave my truck there, and fly back to Inuvik. I thought about that for a minute and realized that my truck would be stuck in Tuk until the barges were running. Now barging a vehicle back to Inuvik would be rather costly, and I would be without my truck. I pleaded my case and said, "You know what. Let me through, please. We will be okay."

He finally gave up trying to turn us back. He took the ribbons down and then came back to my truck with some important rules before we could go on. "First off, you guys need to drive slow through all that water. Go around the geysers as that's the weakest point and that means the ice is cracked right there. Avoid all of them. Also, open up your doors and using one foot keep that door open. If you feel the front of your truck start to fall a bit, jump out of that door and run. Now, take off and I hope you make it back to town with your truck."

I didn't hesitate for a second. Off we went pushing water. We drove as instructed. It was slow going as water was shooting up all around us through the cracks in the ice. At this point, Harry had seen enough. He wanted me to stop and let him out, as we were in water for a long ways ahead yet. He wanted to walk way around through the snow and meet us on the other side of this huge water spot.

I stopped. He got out and off he went walking around the water. Lois stayed with me as she was about 5 months pregnant with Scott, and couldn't have made it all that way in the snow. She and I continued on dodging the shooting up water as best we could. We could feel the ice under us was a bit spongy, to say the very least. I was thinking right about now that with enough whiskey in a fella's belly, anything is possible… too bad Harry drank rum!

I do have to admit that a few times I almost bailed out of the truck, because with me holding my door open with my left foot, and Lois holding her door open with her right foot, water was coming into the truck a lot faster than we liked to see.

After what seemed like forever, we finally made it through the worst of the overflow and were back on ice that wasn't heaving up and full of cracks with water shooting straight up into the air through them. We drove a bit further just to be safe from what was now behind us, and then stopped the truck to see where Harry was. Good thing we had good eyes, as he was not even close to getting all the way around when we finally spotted him.

We felt safer right where we were so we decided to wait for him there. But, as we waited we noticed that water was starting to surround us…damn this was melting fast! It was a good hour maybe a bit more, before Harry got to us in the truck. He was tired and sweating from slogging through the deep snow, and he needed a rum!

We did make it back to Inuvik a bit drunk, and with a bit more respect for the ice road. Harry got some exercise along the way. A trip that should have taken us only 4 hours there and back, loading included, took us 7 hours. It was supposed to be a fun drive to Tuk and back. It was fun all the way there, but coming back, not so much!

HERE KITTY KITTY

Like I mentioned in a previous story, our possessed cat that we adopted never did seem quite right in the head, and that made him a devil cat. If a dog was not right in the head, you usually, over time, can still train it somewhat to be a decent dog. Now I dare you to try training a cat. Even if it's a good cat, it can't be trained! This cat of ours was proving to be more than a handful around its new home. He was actually training us, it seemed… very odd we all thought.

The trailer we were living in was just your usual stick-built trailer, with a good sized living room, decent sized kitchen, and off the kitchen was the hallway to the bedrooms and bathroom. Brian P.'s bedroom was the first room on the right looking from the kitchen down the hall. Then, there was another bedroom on the right for company, and the bathroom. Our bedroom was at the back and if our door was open we could see straight down the hallway into the kitchen. Now picture that in your head and all will make sense as this story unfolds.

Our usual Friday nights were spent between the Legion and the Mackenzie, drinking as much as my wallet would allow for the night. Normally, we would come back home after closing time, and stay up for a few drinks with Brian P. before going to bed. We would be at pre-pass out which usually meant you were almost sleep drinking between talking. Once in bed and within minutes of your head touching the pillow, passing out would come quick. This night was much the same.

Around 4:00 am, I found myself waking up to the weirdest feeling. As I became more aware, I felt something between my legs. What was this? Lois looking for some action was my first thought. That was until I heard her snoring slightly and sound asleep beside me. I pulled the covers back and, at the same time, turned on my lamp by the bed. Right there between my legs was the cat, licking me!

I grabbed that damn cat and actually threw it away from the bed quickly. Lois was still sleeping and I didn't need her to know about this damn cat's new toy. I wasn't sure if the cat was just prepping its food with saliva before it was going to grab a bite of meat balls…after all this thing was possessed!

I managed to get through all of Saturday without saying a damn word about me and the cat. It was something nobody would ever find out. I was no fool. If one person in Inuvik besides me knew, then the entire town would know within 24 hours. These small northern communities were always looking for a good story about anyone, and everyone was a target. I didn't want this one to get out, so I kept my mouth firmly closed… as did the cat, after I had a chat with it.

Saturday found us back at the Legion for happy hour drinks

and games. Then around 11:00 pm, a bunch of us younger folk headed over to the Mackenzie Hotel, or "the Zoo". The usual gang of people were slowing making their way to the bar. It was filling up quickly as was the norm on weekends. This night was uneventful with no rowdiness or fighting, so no new bruises on this body tonight… whew!

Lois, Brian P. and I headed for home at closing time, so that we could have a couple more drinks and tell stupid stories to each other, but I still didn't mention a thing about that damned cat. We all had our limit for the day (I knew we were at our limit when the bottle was empty), and soon we were in bed, passed out.

I couldn't believe what was waking me up once again at 4:00 am. Again, I felt the weird feeling between my legs. I threw the covers off in my half-asleep state, and yes…there was that devil cat licking its food before it takes a bite. I grabbed that cat and tossed him back on the floor. I'm sure I could hear him hissing and growling under its breath as it made its way out of the room heading for the kitchen.

Shit, now that's two nights in a row, and I still can't tell anyone. I dare not say a word. This is between me and that damn cat.

Waking up Sunday with a severe hangover was pretty normal for a good portion of Inuvik. I didn't want to be left out, so I did my best to keep those numbers up. I was successful once again. Sundays are usually reserved for laying around and groaning and moaning and holding your head together before it implodes. All three of us were feeling the effects of the two nights of drinking. It was a good shift and we were feeling like crap. Being young at the time was a blessing. Even on days like these, if you wait a few hours while drinking beer and juice, the cobwebs do go away, but so does your common sense!

The three of us were sitting around and really starting to feel alive again. We continued drinking, thinking it would make us feel even better than it already had. Now this is where my common sense went somewhere. I didn't have it anymore, and I don't know where it went. But I found myself telling Brian P. and Lois about what that cat had been doing the last two nights. I told them everything! It just came out and I couldn't stop talking…damn beer and juice!

Now they were both laughing and bugging me about this. "Sure you stopped the cat," they said. "Yeah, I believe you," as they smirked and winked at each other. Damn. I have literally let the cat out of the bag…the whole town will know by daybreak on Monday.

It turned out to be another long day, mostly because both kept bugging me about how much I loved the cat, all the while pretending to hate the damn thing. There were various other comments, lots of those in fact. Day drinking turned into night drinking, and slowly they seemed to be leaving me alone, finally. We all had to go to work the next day, so it was an earlier night to bed compared to the two previous ones. Lois and I were down at the end of the hall in our room and Brian P. was in his room up on the left from us. We closed our door and Brian P. closed his, as we all said our goodnights.

Lois and I had just gotten into bed when we both heard someone talking quietly. Did we leave the TV on? What the hell? I get out of bed and quietly open my door a bit. I see the back of Brian P.'s head poking out of his room, as he is looking towards the kitchen. He can't see me unless he turns right around, so I wait a second or so, then I heard him talking.

I had a hard time holding back my laughter when I heard what he was saying. "Here Kitty Kitty. Here Kitty." Brian P. heard my muffled laughing and his head spun around. Our eyes met and then he retreated back into his room. We were all laughing hysterically. Now, I had something to tell everyone if the cat got out of the bag.

The devil cat

PRACTICAL JOKE GETS REROUTED

Summer in Inuvik was a bunch of fun with some chaos thrown in. The sun is up 24 hours, and the new warmth brings out all the coatless people. Finally, we can truly see what people look like without being bundled up in big parkas with fur around the face to ward off the bitter cold of the winter months! This time of year also brings out the very best in the practical jokers at work. We were happy for summer for many reasons. Yes, even work was better in summer than winter, for sure!

This story is not so much about the Inuvik weather, but the world of practical jokes in the workplace. Walt was our boss at the time. Guy was our salesman. He got to go out of the building to look after customer orders. In doing so, sometimes, he would be gone from the office for a few hours at a time. Guy was also one of the devious ones when it came to practical jokes, kind of like being the King of the Jokers! He would pull no punches when going after someone, and he always got his intended target…always! Today was pretty busy, and on busy days our guard was down. It was easy to catch someone in a practical joke trap on a busy day.

Guy was being his usual busy self this day, walking briskly back and forth from his desk to the coffee machine, getting work done in between. My desk faced Guy's desk. The only thing between us was one of those cheap high desk dividers that most offices used back in the day. It was cheaper than building other offices with walls, I guess. I could hear Guy, but I couldn't see him from my desk. We were only separated by a panel.

On this particular day, Guy seemed to be busier than the rest of us. This should have been a red flag, but what the hell, he normally is busier to some extent. Now that I look back on this day, I should have known he was up to no good, but 20/20 vision only works in hindsight, not in the moment!

Guy was in his normal work clothes in our dusty little office trailer. He also had a suit in a bag, hung up away from the dust. Dust would take over the office in the summers. Lots of road dust would find its way in. We swept more than once a day just to stay ahead of the mess.

The morning went by pretty fast with no practical jokes on anyone; like I pointed out, it was a busy day. That morning we didn't have time to even think about a way to get someone. I didn't have a plan at all, so I was assuming nobody else did either. How stupid of me!

The clock was at 12 noon and we were all getting ready to head to the Legion for a soup and sandwich. Guy stayed back saying he was much too busy for lunch. That was another missed red flag! We left him sitting at his desk with a promise of bringing him some food, then we all took off for town. Our work was about a five-minute drive from town. We were out in the industrial section on the way to the airport. When lunch was done, we headed back out to the store with our bellies full, and with a bag lunch for Guy.

When I came through the door that separates the warehouse from the office, I noticed Guy sitting at his desk and rummaging through papers acting all busy, but something seemed off. This was another red flag, but I caught this one though! I went over to my desk, but I didn't dare sit down. I could sense Guy was up to something, and I was thinking I was the intended target.

Remember, I pointed out that we worked in a pretty dusty environment? Our floor was usually covered in dust. No matter how many times we swept, it would just keep finding a way inside. This was going to prove to be my saving grace.

My spider senses were tingling; I knew if Guy had his sights set on an intended target, it's game over. He always got his man, or woman. I was getting worried and a little afraid to sit down across from him yet. I needed to visibly go over every single item on my desk and check to see what had been moved since I went to lunch.

Damn, I can't seem to find anything amiss at all. Maybe the red flag was just my own conscience getting to me... overthinking perhaps! I was taking far too long searching my desktop for anything that might show me what I need to know. It was getting awkward, time wise. I should be sitting at my desk by now. I could hear Guy getting fidgety on the other side of the divider. I finished my visual inspection and all items looked perfect, so I pulled my desk chair out to sit down and get to work.

What's this I see right below my chair? It is one little drop of wet in the dust on the floor. How the hell did that get there?

Red flag again and caught! I quietly bent down and looked under my desk. From there I saw all I needed to see.

What really caught my well-trained eye was a clear Bic pen with the guts removed, taped up under my desk with the pointy end facing where my lap would be if I was sitting in my chair. The other end had a hose taped to the bottom of my desk leading back towards Guy's. It was attached to a big 3 gallon pressure hand pump sitting on the floor beside him. His hand was on the pump handle in the ready position.

I started to panic. I needed time to think about what I had to do so that I wouldn't get soaked by that pump. The pressure coming through that Bic pen would likely cut paper, and it was pointed right at my crotch. I moved away from my desk and went up to the front counter to do nothing else, but buy a bit of time before Walt would be yelling at me to sit the hell down.

When doing a practical joke with this crew, timing was everything. Today was no exception, and I now know why Guy didn't come for lunch. He was setting up this elaborate "pen shooting water into groin area"… my groin area… prank!

I had only been up at the front counter for a few short minutes when the phone rang. Walt grabbed that call and it happened to be the purchaser from the hospital. The call was quickly over and Walt came out from his office and told Guy the purchaser needed him at the hospital to go over a quote he had done for them. Walt said, "Guy, put your damn suit on and get over there right away." This is where timing is everything. This is where karma helps, and this is what all the red flags were for. It was my turn to shine!

Guy walked out grumbling a bunch of shit under his breath and didn't seem happy to be leaving the office. I now sat down in my chair. I made sure he witnessed that before leaving, so maybe that was why his blood pressure seemed a bit high! I waited until he had left the yard in the work truck before I started forming what was going to an epic practical joke. Just my luck, it was already set up for me! All I really needed to do was take the tape off that pen under my desk, move it under Guy's desk and aim it at where his crotch would be, and tape it back up. There. I was done in less than 5 minutes. Now I can sit in relative safety while I wait for Guy to come back from the call he went on.

Guy had been gone for damn near 2 hours. He must have been itching to get back as soon as possible, so he could get me soaking wet with his plan, and it was a good plan! Plans change, though, and you have to adapt on the fly some days.

Finally, the swinging door leading to the warehouse swung open and there was Guy, still in his suit. He noticed me sitting at my desk as I pretended to talk on the phone. He actually sped up, to what I would call a step below a full-on run to his desk. He couldn't wait to get me while I was on the phone. He really liked his plan. I could tell by the look in his eyes.

Guy sat in his chair and didn't waste a second. He hit the handle to release the wave of water coming out of that Bic pen. The swearing and screaming coming from the other side of the divider was all I needed. I managed a direct hit on the person who had set up their own practical joke. Guy was mad as hell and jumped up from his desk, because:

1. He was still in his suit and now it was soaked.
2. He spent an entire lunch hour setting this all up so I would get soaked.
3. For once he did not get his "intended target."
4. He became the victim to his very own practical joke!

It just doesn't get any better than that in the practical joke world. That little spot of water in the dust below my desk was all it took to change plans. I am still proud to say that I was the one who got the "King of the Jokers" title at work that day. Sorry Guy, but somebody has to be the one!

Randy Day (left) with his friend Guy (right)

IF YOU HAVE TO PEE...

Whenever my wife, our son, Scott, and I were going to the lake on one of the few weekends that summer gave us, we would always take a few people with us in the boat. It wasn't much of a boat. It was a Lund 18ft open boat, with no top, not much of a windshield, uncomfortable seats, and had a 70hp mercury motor on it. It wasn't much to look at, but over the few years that we owned the little boat, we managed to put a lot of miles on her going back and forth to the lake (90 miles one way).

I had a bad feeling about this trip right from the start, but back then I never did listen to my feelings much. Thinking like that would just cause a guy to drink more, if that was even possible!

We had been planning all week to leave on Friday right after work. We were lucky enough to have our friend, Scruff, the best co-captain I ever had, in the boat with us. I felt much safer with him onboard. Also making the trip with us was our good friend, and my boss at the time, Guy. He was always fun to be around.

After what seemed like a very long week, Friday finally came and it brought some nasty winds with it. The mighty Mackenzie River was rolling with whitecaps thundering into the boat launch area. We didn't like our chances of getting out on the river from there at all, so we decided it wasn't worth spilling our drinks just to try and launch out into the waves like that. We did have one other option to launch from when the wind was coming from that direction, so off we went.

We arrived at the little pond that was mostly out of the wind. It even had a small channel, just the right size for our boat, that would lead us back to the river. We were happy that we were hitting the big waves from a better angle... less spillage... so far so good!

As we were fighting our way through the waves and coming up to where we first thought of putting the boat into the river, I see through my water covered glasses what looks like a person standing up on high ground. As we get right across from this person, he is quite plainly shaking his finger at us and moving his head from side to side. It was my Uncle Dick, and he was trying to get us to turn around. He was supposed to be headed to his cabin as well. I should mention that Uncle had a way bigger boat, which he chose not to launch in these conditions.

It was very rough water. The waves would come up and hit my windshield just before they hit us in the face. What can I say...we were young, stupid, drunk, and had lots of adventure coursing through our veins. We just lifted our glasses in salute to let Uncle know we understood what he wanted us to do, but we were determined to be heading to the cabin.

When the water was calm, and you didn't break down too often, I could get that boat of ours and all its passengers to the cabin in about three and a half hours. This was going to take much longer, which usually meant much drunker as well. I was happy with my four crew members. I could count on Scruff to see the barge buoys way out ahead of anybody else, as well as watch the river closely for any changes in the water. He was always on the lookout for stumps stuck in the mud and yelling, "Quick turn left (or right). Hurry... just fuckin' turn!"

Guy's job on the boat was to make sure I always had a full rye and coke. He had the hardest task. He was usually way too busy to help with much else. Plus, he was funny as shit to be around...just a cool guy to hang out with. Last, but not least, was my wife. Her only job was to look after Scott (who was inside her floater coat in a snuggly). She would drink a splash of Kahlua with her coffee before we got to the lake, under ideal conditions, which was not the case here. I guess my job was to just drive the damn boat and hope that we would make it to the lake safe and sound, probably wet, but safe and sound nonetheless!

We were really not making very good time. We were just getting battered by the whitecaps out in the middle of the river. Scruff said,"Let's try and drive closer to the shoreline for a while. Not as choppy over there." Holy shit...it worked! We were still not going very fast, but we did not have those huge whitecaps to deal with now. Yeah! Less spillage.

We were only about an hour out of town, but had been in the boat for close to 2 hours. Not bad...we're good! We only had one huge rough spot to try and navigate. Bar C is what the place is called. It is right at the junction where you either turn North to go to Tuktoyaktuk, which is right on the Beaufort Sea, or turn left and in 15 miles of twisting and turning waterways you will eventually end up at the cabin.

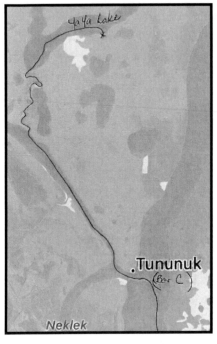

When we finally arrived at the scary crossing, we got totally soaked from the high winds that were sending the waves bashing into our little boat. As a matter of fact, Scruff took on another job halfway across. He was now in charge of bailing water out of the boat as fast as possible!

This patch of water took us a bit of time to navigate as the weather was not helping us much. It was actually slowing our progress down. I think my wife was no longer happy with our decision to leave Inuvik in this shit.

We made it across, but were totally soaked and somewhat cold.

With all bad things, some good must come. We had no sooner made it through to the other side when the wind started to calm down. This would make our trip less stressful, but most importantly, less spillage!

We continued on in our drunken manner, happy that we had made it this far. The cabin was now only about 15 miles away, with just the little channels to travel. The trip was getting better and better as far as any big waves were concerned. This part of the trip was fun to drive the boat in as there were many twists and turns to navigate. I let Guy take a break from filling my cup, so that he could relax a little and enjoy the scenery that these little channels had to offer.

The colours of the Arctic tundra were bright and alive, very beautiful if the winds are not pounding away at you. It took very little time for me to realize that this was just another mistake on my part. Little did I know that the fun was about to stop rather quickly for us.

I had a Texas mickey full of whiskey when we left town, and it was sitting right between Guy and myself. I turned my attention for just a couple of seconds to the big bottle, and started to pump myself another rye when the shit hit the fan.

We were going about 30 miles an hour. In the middle of mixing my own drink, I missed a very crucial turn in the river. Before I knew it, we were hitting the mud and sliding straight off the river and onto the muck. I could only do one thing. Turn the motor off and wait to see how far we were going to go before the boat would come to a stop. Funny thing is, nobody was saying a word. It was very quiet in the boat...too quiet in fact. We stopped sliding on the mud and shore about 100 feet from the water. I calmly stepped out of the boat and said, "Okay everybody that needs a pee...now would be a good time."

Scruff and Guy stepped out of the boat and onto the tundra to have a much needed piss break. My wife just sat in the boat with her arms folded around Scott, not saying a word. Somehow I could tell she was not a very happy camper.

Us three guys finished up our piss break and turned our attention to the boat. After trying to push and pull that boat across the mud and tundra and gaining nothing, we decided the best course of action would be to unload everything, then try and push it backwards to the water. We started to unload the boat, all the while my wife just sat there...not a word coming out of her. I knew she might be just a tiny bit upset, since usually when she was real mad at me she would say so. Things were good when she was only a tiny bit mad...so I thought!

We got everything out of the boat and onto the muddy tundra, except for my wife and our son Scott, who was still in a snuggly thing under my wife's big floater coat. He was safe right where he was and always travelled with us inside that warm coat. The three of us guys started to push, pull and drag that boat towards the water.

Guy says to me, "Do you think Lois is mad at you?"

"Nah, she would be yelling at me if she was. As long as she is quiet, everything is fine."

Guy says, "Do you think she is getting out of the boat?"

"Nope, doesn't look like it!"

Like I said, the wife just sat in the boat not moving and not saying a word the entire time. For a minute there, I almost had myself convinced that she wasn't mad at all. I kept one eye on her, as I'd like to point out that sometimes when I thought she was not very mad, it was quite the opposite. Maybe the whiskey was clouding my judgment just a bit, so I spoke to her. I asked her if she would like to get out of the boat and go behind some bushes to relieve her bladder as we had done...but again silence was all we heard from her!

After quite the struggle, we somehow managed to get the boat back to the water. The three of us made many trips back and forth to retrieve our gear, gas, food, booze, etc. Once it was all packed up again, we pushed off and continued on our way. The cabin was only about 10 miles away at this point. We had not gone very far when the silence my wife had been providing over the last hour or so changed into some of the nastiest words that a world class trucker would have been proud of...me not so much!

This was when I realized I was in a bit of shit. Guy and Scruff picked up on it as well, and now it was the guys' turn to be quiet...but only for a very short time. My two friends could not control the laughter that was festering inside of them. They were laughing pretty hard and bugging me about missing that turn on the river. All I could answer with was, "Hey guys, all I needed was a pee break and that looked like the best place to stop for one...kind of like a rest stop on the highway where you have to pull off the main road."

We did make it to the cabin with everything still intact except my wife's sense of humour. I learned a valuable lesson that day and from then on. I never poured my own drink again. Hell, that was Guy's job, not mine!

In all the years of travelling those 90 miles from Inuvik to Uncle Dick's cabin, we never stopped at that spot for a piss break ever again. Over the years, following that trip up and onto the mud and tundra, there was always somebody in the boat that would remind me of the time that I had parked my boat so far from the water just to have a piss break. That always brought a bit of a smile from me... from my wife, not so much!

Randy and Lois' first boat and the one Randy rode up onto the mud in this story.

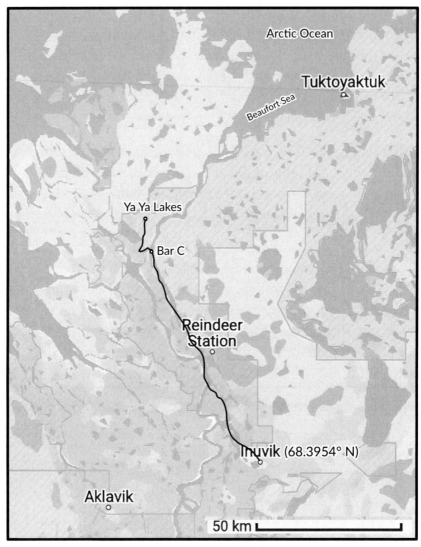

Larger perspective of location of Ya Ya Lakes from Inuvik.

MY ONLY WHALE HUNT

One of my good friends in Inuvik was Richard. He was just one of many in his family that had been up north for their entire lives. They were born and raised and lived off the land for years and years. Those early times must have been tough on everybody. Being Inuit had its benefits and its downsides in this vast land of bitter cold in the winter, and sometimes even the summers were kind of cold as well.

Finding and getting food off the land for the communities was a community effort in the good old days, and still goes on to this day. An example of how well this works for everyone can be seen just outside the community of Tuktoyaktuk where food is stored in a pingo. Pingos are just massive, and can be seen for miles. There is more than one up here by the Arctic Ocean (Beaufort Sea). Simply put, they are just a mound of earth covered ice that can reach up to 230 feet in height and up to 2000 feet in diameter. These huge mounds have been pushed above ground level by the massive strength of the heaving permafrost.

The community refers to the pingo closest to town as their "community freezer". To get to the freezer part, you have to walk down a very sketchy stairwell, that takes you to the inside of this huge chunk of earth and ice. Yes, it is hollow inside.

Once in the middle of this natural freezer you see ice hanging over top of you. This is normal. Also, you will see all kinds of wild meat that has been harvested from the land and sea. It is the job of all the hunters to bring their bounty of food and store it inside. The notion here is the hunters who put food in, can take their choice of food out and share with their families. This system works very well if you can make it down that rickety and scary staircase.

Everyone who is able must contribute. If you were a fisherman, you added fish, seals, walrus and whale to the freezer. A hunter would add caribou, moose, geese, ptarmigan, etc. This way the elders in the community could get food from here without having to go and do the hard work of getting food from the land.

Let's get back to my good friend Richard. He was one of the many young hunters - the gathering of foods guys! The two of us were talking in the Legion one afternoon and he mentioned that he was going to Tuk the next weekend to go whaling off the coast. They were going to look for Beluga whales. That got my attention right away and I thought I'd like to see that happening. I expressed my excited desire and pleaded with him to take me along.

My excitement was short lived though, as with me not being of Inuit ancestry, it was almost impossible to go whaling, even just to watch. Richard explained all that to me and I was bummed

MY ONLY WHALE HUNT

out to say the least. He said he would check with the other hunters to see if I could come along to watch if I stayed out of their way.

Two days later Richard calls me up and says he will pick me up on Saturday. We are going whaling! Wow! That was great news for me. Even just getting out on the ocean in a nice big boat would be fun, I thought.

The days dragged on for me as my excitement grew. This was going to be a huge amount of fun for me, but for Richard and the others it was work. Upon arriving in Tuk, I didn't see any big whaling boats as I had imagined would be in the harbour. There were just a few 14-18 foot Lund fishing boats lined up along the shore. "Ummm," I thought. "Where is our boat?"

Once we parked the boat we had come from Inuvik in, Richard walked towards a couple of other fellas standing beside one of those 18 foot Lund fishing boats. They had no top and no windshield, not even pillows to sit on those wooden uncomfortable seats, but this was our whaling boat.

I was introduced to the others and they seemed happy to have me come along to watch. I wasn't allowed to touch anything, or help in any way, they said. I was good with all that, as I stared at that wee little boat and that huge ocean in front of me. This was the first time I had been to Tuk and had never seen so much water and waves! I was a prairie boy from Manitoba, after all.

Suddenly, deep inside me, I was hoping that the whaling was not good that day. I couldn't swim a single stroke. My only hope was heading straight to the bottom and then run to shore. Many other anxious thoughts ran through my mind too. I was secretly terrified.

We pushed off from shore and out into the waves we went,

bouncing a bit here and there. "Not my idea of fun," I was thinking to myself, while smiling and nodding at each of them. They were calmly making a plan amongst themselves, deciding where to go in order to find a beluga for the community pingo freezer, which was back on solid ground, no waves, just solid ground...oh how I missed that already.

Everybody in the boat had a job to do except me. We went in the direction that the guy sitting up front pointed out to the guy in the back driving. I think Richard's job was to keep me out of the way, mostly.

What seemed like forever, bouncing from wave to wave, the guy up front points off to our left and yells, "Whale!" Well, that got my blood circulating, as I could see we did not have enough room in this boat for all four of us plus the whale. "Could these guys not see that part?" I wondered.

As instructed, our driver headed in the direction of the whale. In a matter of a few minutes, we could see the whale coming up and going back down, right there in front of us. The next step in the process just plain scared the shit out of me.

Once we got close to this big mammal, it was Richard's turn to get to work. He grabbed his rifle, and he fired at the whale. The guy up front threw a spear, with a long rope and a big orange bobber attached, into the whale. After all the commotion and excitement in the boat had settled down, we boated over to this gigantic water monster, so that Richard could put it out of its misery.

Things were beginning to come clear for me. The hunters started grabbing big hooks and more rope while we were bobbing up and down right beside the whale. They quickly, with very little talk amongst them, tied that big bugger right up to our boat. It was slightly longer than the boat and looked huge to my already bulging eyes. A big round of congrats was given between them, while I sat and watched in awe at what I had just witnessed. After all that, the driver started heading back to Tuk with only one catch…one very big catch, in fact!

Once back on shore, and with the whale moved onto solid ground, I was feeling ecstatic about this entire adventure, or maybe I was just glad to be back on dry land. It seemed like the entire village came down to watch us and to help out where needed. But before any help was needed, there was just one thing left to do with this whale. This thing, I had not been told about.

Apparently, if a person, such as I, was allowed to go in the boat and food was brought back, then there was an Inuit ritual that says everybody gets a small cube of fresh, uncooked whale blubber to eat from the bounty. As luck would have it, any person who is invited to go on these whale hunts must eat the very first piece. This piece was only about 3 inches by 3 inches square. "How bad could that be?" I thought. I was more than happy to eat the first piece, as I felt like part of the hunting group now.

I pop that little piece into my mouth and began to chew. The first chew brought a taste that is hard to explain, and there was no way more chewing was making it go away. In fact, with every chew, that same bitterness and terrible tasting junk flooded to the back of my throat. It was horrible and still is. I'm still not sure that taste of whale blubber will ever leave me.

The two good things that came out of this was the community got some much-needed food for the freezer, and I got smart about never ever going on a whale hunt again. As they say about some things, one time is enough.

KETCHUP AND WALT

Working with the crew of people we had in the store, you always had to be watching your back, your sides, and your front. You also needed to pay attention to above. You just never knew when a well-timed practical joke would appear out of nowhere.

This was what work was supposed to be like. Everybody always got their work done, but everyone also seemed to have the time for the perfect practical joke. I think we all loved our jobs. Phoning in sick was not an option. As a matter of fact, all of us could hardly wait to get to work in the morning just to see what might happen that day.

The one thing you learn as a practical joker is there is a huge difference between the "intended target" and the "victim". Sometimes, a well-thought-out practical joke targeting one co-worker would not necessarily get the person you wanted. Someone else would walk into the ambush, which would set off a whole new chain of events. Often it was even better when someone else would get the hit. They would have no idea who set them up, even though they were not the intended target. So yeah, it could get crazy trying to figure who was getting who most days.

This particular morning our boss Walt, Guy, Wayne, Judy, Pike, and me were in the office. Today was going to be epic. I had in my head the plan for the perfect practical joke. Guy was my intended target. I didn't need much set up time, just a few minutes alone in the bathroom. All I needed was a sharp utility knife, a few toothpicks, and some little packs of ketchup that you can get from any restaurant. Pretty simple, but quite possibly the best joke, with the least amount of set up time and items needed to accomplish the task.

Guy was my intended target on this day, but I was willing to catch anybody, except Judy or Walt. "Never get the boss" was an unwritten rule in the building. His rule, but we abided by it at all costs...well, mostly all costs. I planned to get Guy, but Wayne or Pike were suitable alternatives.

Everything I needed was in my pants pocket as I made my way into the bathroom, after Judy had already been. I had to act now; I won't be getting her today. Once inside with the door locked, this is what I did. I lifted the toilet seat, broke the toothpicks in half and set them on the toilet bowl so that they were under the seat. I put one on each side of the seat and one right in the front.

Now, I needed to test for the proper height. I lowered the seat down very carefully and rested it on those three toothpicks. I then grabbed the three little packets of ketchup and folded those packets in half. Then, I very carefully took my utility knife and cut a little slit right in the crease of the fold of each one.

125

Again, I slowly lowered the toilet seat so it was now sitting on the toothpicks just high enough that I could slide the ketchup packets under the seat beside each toothpick. It would be impossible to see unless you actually lifted the seat up. I was hoping to catch Guy when he would be going for his morning crap, just walk in and sit down…great practical joke!

The whole idea behind this was if a person sat down on that seat the following would happen: First, the toothpicks would collapse under the weight. Second, the toilet seat would come down on those three ketchup packs sending ketchup at a high rate all over the intended victim. It just would make a huge mess as the ketchup shot out spraying everywhere. The third thing would be loud swearing and yelling at everyone, from inside the bathroom.

I told nobody what I did before or after, but if they are reading this book, they will now know who did this practical joke. I think after 34 years or so, I should be safe.

I was waiting up on the mezzanine when Guy and our boss, Walt, both went for the bathroom door at the same time right below me. Guy backs away from the door and said, "Go ahead, Walt. I can wait."

"Oh no, fuck me," I'm thinking… "Not Walt, the boss." He was untouchable at work; we were supposed to leave him be. "Oh my." I even started sweating when I watched him go through that bathroom door with his book. Walt was inside that bathroom for a very long time, way too long…what happened? Did he find the packets before he sat down and was wondering what to do? All kinds of thoughts went through my mind.

It seemed like forever to me. I was trying hard to look and act normal so that this joke would not get pinned on me. Walt finally came out and walked back towards his office smiling and not showing any signs of ketchup on him. I was beginning to wonder if my trap had failed. I waited as long as possible, but I just had to go look inside that small bathroom and see if it was covered in ketchup splatter. It took a few minutes, but yes, there was a very tiny spot of ketchup way up high in the corner of the mirror. Success! The ketchup had reached almost to the ceiling! Walt had to have been surprised when ketchup sprayed his lower body and the surrounding walls the second he sat down.

So, you see I had all the makings of a great practical joke… I had the "intended target", but I got a "victim" instead. I hope Walt never reads this; I might not be safe yet!

PIPE BOMBS
AND DRUNK PEOPLE

Well, it seems that working at an industrial supply store, full of cool things, was just the best place to be while living in Inuvik. Yes, we had all the necessary items we needed for our in-house practical jokes, as well as helping us out in our after hours fun… boating included!

Someone mentioned that maybe we should make a bunch of pipe bombs to take to Ya Ya Lake on the next trip. Of course, we all agreed with that crazy idea, and quickly walked out into the warehouse to pick out the necessary items to build the perfect pipe bombs.

Out of the six of us working there at the time, it was only Guy, my cousin, and myself who would be headed to the lake on Friday. We had to start somewhere. After some discussion we decided that a normal black iron pipe schd 40 about ¾ inch around and 4 inches long, full of gun powder would work best. We needed the pipe to be threaded, so that we could put a cap on each end. We would drill a hole in one cap, put the short fuse in the tiny hole, add powder, and then go try it out behind the shop.

While it did go boom (it literally split the pipe in half), both caps stayed on. This made us scratch our heads thinking we needed something else, but what? I think it was Guy's idea to try it the same way, but to use schd 80 pipe, a much tougher, stronger pipe. "What a great idea," we thought. Back to the warehouse we go in search of some ¾ round 4-inch schd 80 pipe fittings with schd 80 caps.

We had just finished building what we thought was a much better pipe bomb, but before we could try it, the store got busy. We didn't have time to test our new product. Because of this, all we did for the rest of the week, when the store was not busy, was build more of those pipe bombs.

Even though the weekends seem like they take forever to arrive, they come and go just like every other week. We had been busy at work, but still managed to build about eight of those little gun-powered-filled noise makers by Friday. Off we went to the lake without testing our newest product. We literally had no idea what these little ¾" x 4" black pipe bombs were capable of. Were we worried about that little detail? Not at this time! Drinking and getting to the cabin, while having fun, was first and foremost on the agenda.

The trip to the lake was great. Not much wind was stirring up the Mackenzie; it was just sun and wind in our hair. With these conditions, my boat could usually get to the cabin in about three and a half hours, which was about the same amount of time it took to drink a full 26oz bottle of whiskey for me…and me alone.

I always had a 40oz in the ready position for when we arrived at the cabin.

So, getting back to our little pipe bomb experiment. We decided that we wouldn't mention them to the other people up at the cabin this beautiful summer evening. The booze was flowing as was normal most nights on any given weekend, so waiting one more night would not be a problem.

Waking up extremely hung over on a Saturday was normal to all of us. Most mornings started off with Bailey's and coffee with our breakfast, then a few beers and juice, followed quickly by well-made Caesars. Then, it would be whiskey time, once again, unless Uncle needed a project started or finished. If nothing needed doing, then back to the fun of a beautiful Saturday at the cabin….and our secret pipe bombs.

On this weekend there were more people than the cabin slept, so a couple of tents were pitched on the beach down in front of the cabin for the overflow of bodies. I guess we had 14-16 people hanging out with us… some regulars, some first timers.

Just to make things clear, the cabin was about 30 yards from the lake with about 20 yards of sandy beach in-between. If you were standing on the deck looking out to the lake, on your immediate right there was a 20 foot or so high cliff running all along the beach. The tents were on the beach over on the left a bit from the cabin. It was a perfect day to get those bombs out and have a little fun, hopefully a lot of fun!

We brought out the newest best thing for us. After a bunch of varying reactions towards our tiny bombs, we started to get busy figuring out where to blow them up…and how! After some looking around and lots of talking and drinking, we came up with the idea to put the first one way over in front of the cliffs I mentioned earlier. At this point, at least 10 people were following us everywhere we went.

We finally sat it down and decided to cover it with sand. I believe it was determined beforehand that Guy was our expert on pipe bombs, and almost any bombs. It was Guy who pushed the five-foot-long fuse into the hole in the cap until it was half way through the powder inside. It was also Guy who lit the fuse while the rest of us were already running in all different directions. Picture about ten people running and laughing and screaming all over the beach with no idea where to go.

I was smart and headed straight to the other side of one of the tents. Guy, thinking I was the smart one, came over right beside me. We were even crouched a little as we waited for the boom.

Lois was standing up on the deck of the cabin overlooking the sheer mess of people all over the beach. She yelled down to Guy and myself, "You two do know that if the pipe comes at that tent, it's just like wearing another shirt...eh?" To which both Guy and I turned and stared into each other's eyes, much like the deer in the headlights look.

A picture of the "protective" tents we hid behind (on the Ya Ya Lake beach)

All we could do was say, "Fuck!", just before the BOOM! It was loud! It sounded like it was moving fast…a loud whistling noise that instantly made everyone stop dead in their tracks, statue like.

After the old proverbial dust settled, our initial shock turned to being perplexed. Guy and I ran over and looked at where we had set the loud thing. All we could find was a small hole in the ground…ummm!

We had learned a lot from the very first try, like running won't help, forget tents, and a five-foot fuse is not long enough to find a place to hide. After some talking and head-scratching, we decided we would make a hole in the side of the cliff that faces the lake. We hoped the next one would head out to the water instead of having no idea where it was going to go. We made the hole just deep enough so that all that was showing was the black cap and the ten foot length of fuse… no more five foot ones for us!

Once we packed dirt around our little bomb, Guy once again lit the fuse. Off we all went running, same as before, a bunch of adults running amok trying not to get run over by anyone, or everyone. This time we had more time to find something slightly thicker than a 2-person tent for protection though. And then there it was, the BOOM…followed by that high pitched whistling noise of something flying very fast. I have shot a lot of different guns in my time, and I never heard a noise like that before today. We were excited and eager to get to the hole in the side of the cliff to check out our new bombing area.

Once we got to the spot, it was easy to see a large hole where we had originally put a rather small hole. We dug into the cliff looking for any remains of the boom, only to be confused once again. We found…nothing! We decided that little pipe, caps on and all, shot straight out of the side of the cliff and over the lake at an alarming rate of speed. With still a few of these left we figured the safest place to be playing with our little, but powerful bombs, was right here.

We set another one up but buried it not as deep, leaving two inches sticking out of the cliff. This time another big boom followed by a whistling noise again, but it was not the same. It sounded more like a jet plane out of control...tumbling perhaps, and loud. We had no idea where that one headed, but we looked around to make sure everybody was still standing and not bleeding.

At this point we still had not had enough fun, dangerous fun... Yup! We started scouting for that next spot to set one off. We ended up going up to the top of the cliff. From here we had a perfect view of the area overlooking the lake in one direction, and miles and miles of tundra everywhere else. We were not sure what we were looking for yet, just wandering around looking for something to use with the bomb. Well, it turned out that the perfect thing was sitting right in my uncle's bone yard of junk, stuff that literally had no purpose anymore.

We found an old fifteen-gallon round metal gas can that was rusty inside and no longer safe for holding gas. Sure, it wasn't holding gas at this moment, but the smell was still there. If you smelled where the bung holes were, it was somewhat overpowering. We had decided that this was going to be the last bomb going off today. We still had all our fingers and toes and eyes, no missing parts.

We were quite excited about this old gas can, and maybe a bit nervous, as we had no idea what was going to happen. We put the can on its side, and then put the bomb into the one open bung hole nearest the ground, but only about halfway in. Guy did not want to light this one. We needed somebody fast to light it, then run and jump down on the cliff side out of harm's way. They picked me to be the fast guy. Dang it, I shouldn't have made eye contact… alright then!

I've got this! After everyone was below the top of the cliff, I lit that damn fuse and started running towards them. I jumped off the cliff landing part way down, well hidden from the barrel. I crawled my way back up to where the others were laying with their heads down. After what seemed like a long enough time, there was still no boom. We were getting nervous. Somebody questioned me if I had even lit the fuse, I just told that guy to "go have a look". I was not surprised when he declined my offer. We were getting a bit frustrated as this was taking way too long in our minds, but nobody wanted to take that peek over the top of the cliff in case you got a barrel in the head.

The only thing we had learned up to now was we never had any idea what was going to happen!

While we lay below the top of the cliff, we couldn't see what was going on up top. So, with that we decided that all of us would just look over, like real fast, to see if the fuse was still burning. We had no sooner got our heads above the level of the bank when the much-anticipated BOOM happened.

That barrel lifted off the ground straight up into the air about twenty feet and then came slamming back down to the ground right in front of our eyes. The noise was the loudest BOOM yet, and we all came scrambling up the hill to go check it out. What we found was a barrel, with the top and bottom both blown out round, so now it wouldn't stand on its own. It was like those old punching toys we had as kids; you hit it and it just came right back up to you. This barrel could not stand at all, it was more of a soccer ball than a barrel now.

That's about when Uncle Dick said, "Guys, I think that's enough bombing for today". Funny how we listened when Uncle talked.

We were headed to somebody getting hurt if we would have continued.

That was another fun day at Ya Ya Lakes; lots of good laughs and better yet, no casualties!

TOILET FUNNEL

The second time that I moved back to Inuvik was in the early 1980s. It turned out to be a good decision. Besides, the Brandon City Police even recommended I go. They even suggested that I stay up there for at least 7 years. I won't go into detail around that, but rest assured, I didn't do anything that warranted a jail sentence. It was just some good solid advice given to me while I was in their back seat, with my arms behind me in hand cuffs, on the way to jail! Turns out these two police officers were actually trying hard to save me from the jail system, nice fellas for sure. I took that advice and was a happy camper once I got back to Inuvik.

Arriving back in town, I noticed that things seemed so much busier than when I first went up in 1977, which had a lot to do with why I needed my second trip north. The town was bustling with activity. There were lots of jobs and not enough people to fill them, nothing like the 70s at all. I worked for Northern

Canada Power Corporation for a brief stint until I was offered a job at one of the industrial stores in town. We sold everything from bolts to washing machines during the good times in the oil and gas sectors, and there was lots of action out in the Beaufort Sea with Esso and Beaudrill Drilling, Polar Drilling, and some others that I just don't remember. We worked hard day in and day out; the phones ringing almost nonstop.

We took orders over the phone, then we would package the items up and ship them as quickly as possible. There were also times that the purchasing guys from these companies would come to town. Once in town, those guys would just drop into the store and give us a list, usually a big list, of items needed back out at sea. They would tell us we had two days to fill these lists completely. This was where the washing machines, loafs of bread, anything at all came into play. We became the one-stop shop. After giving us a list of items, the fella would go on a two or three day drunk in town.

I felt pretty lucky to be working at this job, as I was working with lifelong friends; I just didn't know it yet. These friends became very close and we still get together after 30 some years have slipped away on us all. These friends, my co-workers, were the funniest, smartest, most evil and best practical jokers I have ever worked with. In between the phone calls, the walk-in customers, packing up freight, and unpacking freight, these guys were the best. Not quite as good as I was, but a close second.

The co-workers I am talking about are Guy, Wayne, Judy, and my cousin. Today's target for the practical joke I had set up was Wayne. Before I go much further, I need to say that Wayne was almost impossible to get. He was on everybody's radar. Trying to get Wayne took patience, mental toughness, stealth, and the ability to get back into the store after hours to set up the prank. I had all those items checked off. I thought if anybody could get him...it was me!

Our office was an ATCO trailer attached to a very large warehouse where all of our industrial supplies were stored. There was a door leading from the office into the warehouse. Just inside the warehouse, on the left side, was our washroom. There were steps up the back side where we could store items up on the flat roof of that little bathroom. Right across from it, and on the right side of the door, was our mezzanine. We stored all the light stuff there, like metal garbage cans, vehicle filters, etc. From on top the mezzanine, which was slightly higher than the bathroom, you could see the roof of the bathroom. I was up on the mezzanine, looking over at the bathroom roof. I smiled to myself as this plan started to unfold in my head… the one plan that would get Wayne!

Wayne was one of these guys that had a routine for everything whether it be working out, playing hockey, playing baseball, or chores around the house. He did everything the same, everything, even his bathroom breaks. We used to laugh at him because at 10:30 every morning he would head over to that little bathroom so that he could finish processing his food and coffee. This usually took about 4-5 minutes each time.

I knew I was going to have to be stealthy and quick in order for this plan to work. I needed at least an hour to set this one up, which meant coming back to work after we were closed for the day. No problem. I had a key.

The first thing I did was go inside the washroom and measure the distance from the wall to the centre of the toilet, then up I went to the roof with the tape measure, a funnel, some silicone, some clear fishing line, a drill, a jug of water, and a plug for the funnel, with a small eye hook screwed into the plug. I was all set now. I measured the distance, and drilled a hole in the roof that I was hoping would be right above the toilet… right in the middle, if I measured right, was the goal here.

Once I had that part done, and thankful that my measuring was spot on and my hole drilled perfectly, I was on to the next step. I placed the funnel into the hole and put the plug in. Then, I added a bit of water to try this out before I went any further. I was pretty excited when I pulled the plug out of the funnel and the water hit the toilet bowl. Anyone sitting on the toilet would get very wet and surprised; and most likely be scrambling off the toilet with pants around their ankles. That's the vision I had in my mind. I smiled a little at the thought. I could hardly wait until work the next day and that magical 10:30 bathroom break!

But there was still more to do. After my trial run worked so well, I had to go get a ladder and some more hooks, so that I could run the fishing line up from the water filled funnel and over to the top of the mezzanine out of sight…even Wayne's sight. His spider sense was not going to work tomorrow! The fishing line was tucked away nicely and ready for action. All I had to do was be up on that mezzanine at about 10:25 pretending to be doing something, and wait for Wayne to walk into the bathroom. At that point, I would wait a minute or so until he settled down on the toilet. Then, I would pull the fishing line and unleash a full big funnel of water right on top of his unsuspecting head. I could get down off that mezzanine and be back inside the office before he dried off! Again, a stealthy move by me was going to be needed.

It is 10:30am and Wayne's late. I'm actually shaking with anticipation of finally getting this guy. I would never tell anyone that I did it, but I would know, and that's all I needed. 10:35am – I'm still waiting and hoping the boss doesn't come into the warehouse. I was doing nothing but rearranging the garbage cans over and over. "Come on, Wayne."

Is he sick? He is 5 minutes late for his crap… not what I needed right now. 10:40am the door from the office to the warehouse swings open and here comes my target. You cannot even imagine how good I was feeling with the knowledge that I alone have pulled one over on the elusive Wayne. This made it all worth the time spent the night before to set this up.

He doesn't see me up on the mezzanine as he is focused on that bathroom door. I was chuckling to myself and oh so proud of what was about to happen.

Once he closed the door to the bathroom I was waiting. I needed to give him time to be sitting comfy before I pulled that string. The minute I waited seemed like ten agonizing minutes of torture, let me tell you. I was now with fishing line in my hand and within seconds of the best practical joke yet! I yanked the string hard, the cork popped out, the water fell fast and I was elated with myself.

I heard Wayne yell from the bathroom, "Nice try, Zip, but you missed!"

What? How was that possible? What kind of trick is he trying to play on me? How the hell did he even know it was me? I was stealthy, fast, and perfect in every way. By the time Wayne got out of the bathroom, I was inside the office mingling with our co-workers who had no idea what I had done…yet! I am still dumbfounded. What went wrong? I had thought of everything. All these thoughts were going through my head when into the office walks Wayne, big smile and walking like a proud mom with her first baby, and not a drop of water on him…nothing!

Inside that little bathroom was a small water heater where the reading material is kept. It's not really in arms reach from the toilet, especially for a short fella like Wayne. As it turned out, while I was waiting to pull the fishing line, Wayne had been sitting on the toilet. He stood up to get a magazine from the little heater just as I pulled the string sending a stream of water into the middle of the toilet right behind him, missing him completely.

"Oh, NO!" I thought quietly. How come he is so hard to get? Why did he call my name when I missed? How did he get out of there and not be wet? These were all questions I couldn't even ask, because then he would have known for sure it was me. The first and most important thing about practical jokes…never let on it was you. Try to put the blame on anyone else if possible.

That was the end of the toilet funnel trap. Everyone would check that roof before they went in and sat down.

A perfect trap was avoided once again by the "spider sense" of my good friend Wayne. There was always time to try something else another day. At least, that was my hope!

PTARMIGAN MATING DANCE

It was closing time at the Legion on a nice sunny spring Saturday night in Inuvik. We weren't quite ready to go home yet, so the four of us, Uncle Dick, Guy, Brian P., and myself, decided to go for a drive. We got our shotguns and some travelling cocktails and went for a drive down the Dempster highway. With the long days, we had enough light to hunt for ptarmigan and rabbits to put into the freezer. Needless to say, and just so there is no confusion here, our wives were mad as hell at us for going on our little drive. We had just spent most of the entire day playing pool, throwing darts, and bull shitting in the Legion. But, we just couldn't pass up such a nice night to go for a drive and a hunt, though it was more about sharing some more cocktails and laughs than anything else.

It took us about half an hour to get our stuff together and off we went down the highway. It was about 2:30 in the morning by the time we hit the outskirts of town. We had the highway all to ourselves at that time of the night. The sun was still up and all four of us were happy to be out enjoying some more time together, while maybe getting a chance at some birds and rabbits.

I guess we picked the right night as we had not gone very far before we had a couple of ptarmigan and a rabbit in the back of the truck. "So far so good," we thought. The ptarmigan were still in their winter white colour, so they were very easy to spot in the bushes on both sides of the Dempster, even from a distance. The rabbit hunting was also going pretty well. It seemed like each time we stopped to shoot, rabbits would go running and jumping, giving away their hiding spots and leaving us no choice but to get some for the freezer.

At one point we came across two ptarmigans that were right in the middle of what can only be described as their mating ritual. My uncle, who has lived off the land his entire life, jumped out of the truck with shotgun in hand and took careful aim.

He stopped just short of shooting, and with Brian P. and myself standing right beside him, he started to talk all sentimental, like I have never heard him before. He said, "Hey guys, look at this. Here is something that a lot of people don't get to see. This is what nature is all about…just look at these two ptarmigan. They are right in the middle of their mating dance," he said. "Wish we had brought a camera. Take a moment and watch this, as we may never get the…"

All of sudden there was the loud, unmistakable sound of a shotgun going off and both ptarmigan crumpled up and fell over dead. We were kind of stunned by the noise and quickly turned to see Guy standing there with shotgun in hand and with a little grin on his face. He says, "There… they are fucked now, Dick!"

143

A WALK IN GRIZZLY COUNTRY

This weekend up at Uncle Dick's cabin was much the same as most weekends, except for this one little thing.

This weekend, in particular, started out just like all the rest when heading up to the cabin. I try to get off work on Friday as early as possible, go get the truck and boat which was already hooked up and ready to put the boat in the water, and put my boating clothes on over top of my 357 handgun that was strapped to my waist under my coat, a must have when travelling the Mackenzie River on any day. Then, I loaded the truck with our groceries, and loaded up the booze we needed to make it through a weekend. Once all that was done, we were within hours of leaving the dock to start heading north to the cabin. But we still had one stop to make on the way to the water, the Legion!

We always stopped at the Legion before shoving off onto the river as Del, the nice lady bartender, would let us fill a couple of 5 gallon orange Gott coolers with ice from their cooler for our weekend. We were always so happy to get that ice, which we needed at the cabin as much as we needed food. Who wants to drink warm whiskey, or scotch, or rum?

Remember when I said we were within hours of leaving the dock? Well, once we were inside to get the ice... you just can't take it and go. With the sun up for 24 hours, we were never in any rush to leave the Legion. Funny how you wait all week to go up to the cabin and then spend anywhere from one to six hours bull shitting with everyone, playing darts, shuffle board, or drinking games up at the bar. Hell, there was plenty to do at the Legion, so no need to be in a rush leaving this little piece of heaven.

But all good things do come to end, and off we went to the river to put the boats in the water. Yes, boats. Some weekends, we would have five or six boats heading up to Ya Ya Lake to the cabin. Uncle always said, the more people that come up, the more people that can help. I think he really meant the more people to party with for Friday and Saturday, and a bit on Sunday, before we would have to head back to town. Unless, of course, the weather was bad and the crashing of the waves onto the beach would leave our boats high and dry...and that happened a lot. "Storm-stayed" we called those little ripples some weekends, which gave us an extra day at the cabin and not in town working.

An example of a storm coming in at Ya Ya Lake.

145

I spent many weekends, and many years, travelling that big river, always with my handgun, a shotgun, and also my 8mm rifle. If you ever broke down between town and the cabin, you could be rest assured that you will see signs of a bear nearby, no matter where you stopped along the river banks. You had to keep yourselves safe on every stop, planned or unplanned.

After all the trips I took back and forth, weekend after weekend, year after year, there was this one spot that I always said I wanted to stop at. You could, from the river, just make out what looked like an old camp set up about 300 yards from the river up on a little rise. There was even a half-grown walking trail through the waist high shrubs and bushes. I thought, "Hey, this Saturday with most everybody hung over from the Legion and partying at the cabin until the wee hours, we should go for a boat ride to gather some wood along the river banks for those cooler fall weekends." I managed to talk three others into coming with me. So, the four of us set out in my boat to hunt wood. I had Brian P., Charlie, as well as my boss, Guy, with me for this job.

After leaving the lake and getting into the river channels, we just started cruising along nicely watching the shoreline for wood. While having a few drinks and some good laughs, this group of friends in the boat were kind of funny from time to time, and this was one of those times. We managed to get some wood, considering we were driving slow, but drinking fast. It was by accident that we just happened to be driving by that special spot I had always wanted to see, but was always in a hurry to either get to the cabin or get back home. Today we were going to change that.

I guided the boat over to what looked like a natural landing spot to tie up the boat so that the current wouldn't drag it out to the water leaving us high and dry. We all got out of the boat, and

146

tied it up good. Then, we each grabbed our rifles and shotguns, plus two of us were packing 357 handguns...yes that seems like a bit much, but if you have ever lived way up in the northern part of our country, you would understand our need to be careful. Bears are smart and so were we...or so we thought!

Without a care in the world, the four of us walked up that overgrown trail all the way to the spot where that old canvas tarping and some bits of rotten wood surrounding that canvas were...and that was it. All those trips back and forth, thinking this was something special enough to take time to go walk up the 300 or so yards from the river and see...nothing really!

We all figured it was a waste of time and our time would be better spent on getting some more wood, as that is what Uncle Dick wanted us to do in the first place. "No sense wasting gas for nothing," he would say. When the gas station is 90 miles away, you had to use the fuel wisely.

The four of us had just started back down the trail when each of us stopped dead in our tracks, and just stared at each other. There was now a very strong smell of what we all agreed was what a bunch of dead rotten things would smell like. It was overpowering to the point that we knew we were smelling a grizzly bear. This smell was not on the trail when we walked up to this spot, but now the stench was awful to breathe in. It was a "hold your nose" kind of smell... the worst smell I have ever encountered. It was just bad.

Then, the hair on our necks stood up. We realized we were in huge trouble right then. We were 300 yards from the boat and going to have to walk back down with the waist high shrubs pretty close to us on both sides, the entire way to the boat, knowing that a bear was right beside us...in those shrubs.

With all of us carrying a loaded rifle with a sling over our shoulders and shotguns in hand with the plugs out and loaded, with five shells each, I made a game plan in a hurry. "Think big," I thought. I said to the guys that for the walk back we needed to have two guys facing forward walking slowly. The other two guys would have their backs pressed against the forward-looking guys, walking at the same pace, so that our backs would not come apart. We took the safety's off our shotguns and got ready to shoot whatever came out of those shrubs.

At this point, the four of us were equally terrified, just from that overpowering rotten smell. Knowing we were in a bind, we slowly started back down that trail with heads turning and looking and wondering what was following us, as the smell was staying with us. I have smelled a skunk that just sprayed, and that will make your eyes water. This smell was much worse.

As we made our way hopefully to the safety of my boat and the open water…that damn smell just kept following us like a big rotten cloud all around us…very pungent, awful in fact. That walk took forever, it seemed. When you are back to back and slow, 300 yards seems like miles.

As we all walked towards the boat, not once did any of us say a word. Once we hit the trail, I believe all of us thought this was the end for us, but at least we will get a few rounds of shells into that beast if the shit hits the fan. After what seemed like an eternity, we arrived at the boat complete with that smell still all around us. He could see us, but we couldn't see him. One guy was untying the boat while the other three kept their weapons at the ready, just in case.

Once in the boat, three guys had their guns out while I was starting the boat and trying to quickly back away from that smell. I must say that I have only been really scared of something maybe three times in my life. This was one of those times. This one little thing changed my desire to ever stop within miles of that spot ever again. We got away lucky that time as we knew grizzlies could be anywhere. I guess now I know what was living up on that spot I needed to see.

Randy "Zip" Day and his Uncle Dick showing how their hand guns would be positioned under their clothes.

OUR WEDDING BOOZE

Lois and I were married in Inuvik, on the front lawn of my aunt and uncle's house.

Lois and I were preparing in advance the food and booze to keep people happy, and not hungry, on our wedding fun day. I was buying extra booze, and it soon became evident that we didn't have enough fridge space at our house. So, Brian P., our full-time roommate and best friend, brought us an extra fridge that we could just dedicate for booze. It was perfect. We moved some things around in the kitchen, so that both fridges would fit without interfering. Then, we filled the borrowed fridge with the booze we had packed so tightly into our fridge. Now, we had one fridge that had extra room for food, and one fridge with extra room for booze. This made us happy. Back then, we were young, and it was little things that made us happy.

Sometimes happy doesn't last. Sometimes things do not go as

planned, and happy can turn into a whole different range of emotions including angry, furious, enraged, startled, shocked, overwhelmed, terrified, just to name a few. All those happened in the same night.

Lois and I were fast asleep in our room at the back of the trailer we lived in. Brian P. had the room closest to the kitchen and front door of our place. It was just a normal Friday night in Inuvik. We had been out to the Legion and Mackenzie Hotel and got back home at bar closing time, as usual! This night we went our separate ways to our rooms. Drunk and tired makes a person pass out, it seems. Normally the three of us would sit up and have a few before bedtime.

I have no idea how I even heard the front door slam shut. We had been home for a few hours and were fast asleep. I did hear it though, and I woke Lois up. We both ran past Brian P.'s room to the front door. It was closed. I could have sworn I had heard it close, so we did a quick check and there was Lois' purse right on the counter by the front door. She looked inside and everything was fine. We were both scratching our heads and wondering what was up. Then, I just leaned over a bit and opened the booze fridge. Damn, there were at least four bottles missing. It was easy to see that as I had them all in order. I was sure of it.

This time of year, the sun is up 24 hours which makes it easy to see if something is going on in the neighbourhood. We both looked out the windows facing the street, but we couldn't see anybody out and about. Our neighbour came to his window and told us that a couple of girls had tried his door, then decided they were at the wrong place. He said they came into our home. We couldn't see anyone around, so we just went back to our room to get some more sleep. Brian P. had not even woken up, yet.

I am guessing we had only been in bed ten minutes when we both heard the unmistakable sound of someone coming up our front steps. We lived high off the ground, as did most people in Inuvik. I had time to run to the front door, while telling Lois to call the cops. I got to the front door and I could hear two women talking while they made it to the top of our landing. I grabbed the door handle, and as soon as I felt it trying to be opened from the other side, I yanked the door wide open to see two very startled, shocked, and drunk women staring at me. I have to say, back then I was not scared of anything or anybody, as I had been trained in judo, as well as karate, and I loved a great fight every now and then.

It only took a mere second or two before they realized they needed to run. Down the stairs they went. I yelled back to Lois, who was on the phone with the police, that I was going after them. By this time, they had a head start on me as they were already at the bottom of the stairs and running fast, but I was faster. By the time I got to the bottom of our stairs, they were running down the middle of the road screaming loudly about something. I was too mad to care about what they were yelling, and just wanted to catch even one of those booze stealers.

I am not far behind them, as they head straight to a house on the other side of the street. I am right on their asses as they get to the door, with me halfway up the steps, mad as hell! Then, shit got real crazy!

A guy from inside opened it up for the girls, and now I can make out what they were yelling. It was something like, "Hey, OPEN THE DOOR! HE'S CHASING US. HELP!" Then, as the door was already open for them, they ran inside. Then, a bunch of guys came out and started running at me.

Now I had a choice to make. I could use my judo skills, and

maybe some karate skills, or my fast running skills and retreat. I had about a second to see which of these three skills I was going to use…I chose to run!

Now I am heading back towards my place very quickly, as Lois watched out the front window. With all this unfolding, Brian P. is still in his room passed out. I was screaming in the general direction of our place for Lois to tell those cops to get here, NOW! These guys were chasing the hell out of me. I ran way faster heading back home than I did chasing those women to the party house.

I was so happy to see the cops coming up the street as I started up my stairs, still running! The guys chasing me also saw the cops, so they headed back to their place very quickly. Whew… sure glad I didn't have to hurt those guys with my other skills. I really wanted them to see how fast I could run. Now they knew!

I went with the two police officers, over to that house, and I thought it was funny how nobody came out to chase the three of us away. As a matter of fact, it took a few minutes before they would even open the door. Once inside, I picked out one of the two girls that had been at our place, but the other one was not there. The police put her in cuffs, then sat her in the back seat of their cruiser. They left me in the front seat, I think just to keep her company and yell at her…so I did both! The two officers went walking around trying to find the other woman, but that proved fruitless. She was long gone.

When the cops got back to the car, I had the name of the other woman and a crying thief in the back seat. Lois was still watching from the window, and Brian P. was still nowhere to be seen. All this from start to finish took at least an hour, so it was a lot of commotion in a short period of time. I had beat up a bunch of guys with my running fast skill; I got the thief to rat out her friend, and now here is the crazy part... The one woman who had gone into hiding that night was a lady that worked with Lois in her office, and had overheard Lois telling one of her friends at work that we needed a fridge for just the booze for the wedding and one for food. They came twice that night to try and get it all, but I totally had things covered... as I'm just fast like that.

Brian P. remained passed out until morning. He missed a fun and crazy night.

UNCLE DICK CALLED OUR CAB

This was going to be a great Saturday. Uncle Dick and I were in the Legion, playing darts and shuffle board, and drinking of course. I may as well tell you that Uncle thought he was the best at all three of those, and I thought I was. We were both very competitive in all three categories! I think I had the edge on the drinking part at least. The darts and shuffle board proved Uncle was slightly better...only slightly, as I did manage to win the odd game here and there.

Uncle was clever and just when you thought you had the upper hand, he would somehow manage to find a way to beat you. He was not only clever, but also pretty sly in letting you think you were going to win. He would just stand back with that little smirk on his face, while I would brag and be cocky about how I was going to beat his ass. At the time it seemed funny. He was in total control, and he usually won no matter how hard I tried.

We had stayed in the Legion from around noon until just about closing time. We decided that heading over to the Mackenzie Hotel before it closed would be a good idea. After all, it was a very short stumble up the street. It would provide another hour, or so, of drinking time for us. I usually had my fill of people by this time of night. I only say night, because of the time. The sun was up and shining bright.

The owner of the Mackenzie Hotel at the time was a fella by the name of Walter. He was a very good friend of my uncle's, and quickly becoming a good friend to me as well. He was always happy to see both of us coming through the door, and he always made room for us no matter how full his bar was.

The Mackenzie Hotel was the roughest bar in Inuvik, and was known around town as "the Zoo", and for good reason. This bar provided countless hours of entertainment. Sometimes we found ourselves right in the middle of a scuffle and had to fight our way out of it. At other times, we would just stand back and watch the fun…that usually hurt less! This night proved to be very entertaining. Uncle and I just stood back watching, while drinking our drinks that Walter gave to us.

Slowly the fighting and yelling started to wind down, as most of the rowdy people took to the parking lot to finish what they had started inside. By now Uncle had made a walk through the bar, and stopped to talk to a few of the people that were left inside. He came back to where I was, informed me that there was going to be a party after the bar closed, and he had the address.

Neither one of us knew the people who were having the party. We didn't let that get in our way as we were still very thirsty and just looking for another place to go. After talking about it, we decided to go and see what kind of fun we could find over there.

Uncle suggested we take a cab over to the party, as we had

156

the address, but had no idea where in town it was. I think our judgment may have been slightly off, but after putting in a full shift of drinking, anything seemed like the right thing to do.

While I stayed with Walter up at the bar doing my best to finish off the drinks I had in front of me, Uncle went out to the pay phone to call our cab. At this time of the night, as the bars around town were closing, it was near impossible to get a cab. They were very busy! When Uncle came back from the lobby where the pay phones were, he had that silly sly smirk on his face and said, "You better hurry and drink up, Randy. Our cab will be here shortly."

"Umm," I thought, "how the hell did he manage to find a cab so quick?" Again, missing a few brain cells, that thought quickly left my mind. I guzzled down my last drink and the both of us said our thanks to Walter, and headed to the front door to wait for the cab.

We had only been standing on the steps outside for a minute or two when a cop car pulls up right at the bottom of the steps. Uncle says to me, "Let's go. Our cab is here." Uncle had tried to get a cab, and was told it would most likely take an hour. As I mentioned, they were tough to find at this time of the night. He had called the police station and asked if they could send a car over for him, as he needed a ride. Somehow this didn't surprise me, as Uncle knew all the RCMP in town pretty well.

When Uncle opened the door of the police car, the driver said, "Hey Dick, where you guys headed?" Uncle gave them the address. They had already heard about that party, and had drove by the street a bit earlier just to check it out. With both of us in the back seat, off we went. Uncle was chatting with the two guys in uniform up front. They even told us the name of the people who lived in the house we were headed to.

Inuvik was not a very big town, and it really didn't take long for the police to get us to our party destination. Upon arriving at the party, the first thing we saw was people outside, lots of them, in fact. The police, instead of letting us out on the road a bit back from the party, just drove right into the driveway and parked in front of everyone.

We did not recognize a single person outside, but they looked like they knew us as they were all staring at us. Some were throwing their lit joints out, some were dumping beer out, and some went running. We didn't let that bother us. We were just happy to be getting there. By the time we got out of our "cab", everyone was gone from the front yard. Some had left while others had retreated inside the house. The two nice officers wished us a good night and waved while they backed out of the driveway leaving us. We headed over to the front door that everyone seemed to run into.

We walked up the steps. The front door was open, and we could hear a bunch of murmuring amongst the people as we walked past. We were headed to the kitchen to try and score a few drinks for us. We didn't bring any as most people will share... most! We did notice that the house was full of people much younger than us, and we couldn't find a face we recognized. Nobody offered us a drink, as we both stood in the kitchen.

More people came from the living room into the kitchen area. We heard someone saying, "Hey, that's the two guys who came in the cop car." All of a sudden, we both realized we were in a very bad spot. We were the guys who brought the cops to a dope and drinking party. There were more and more people standing in place, blocking our path out of this mess we had ended up in.

Things were getting pretty scary now, as people were starting to talk to us, saying shit like, "Why did you bring the cops here?

Are you guys cops as well?" Things were starting to escalate and both of us just wanted to leave. Uncle grabbed the house phone and made a call to our "cab" to hurry back and pick us up. About two minutes later, that cop car was once again parked in the driveway.

The people inside were agitated and nervous as they backed away from blocking our exit to freedom, and the help we desperately needed right then.

As we were getting back into our seats in the back of the car, someone from inside came out on the porch to yell at us. Something to do with us being assholes and working with the cops, among other crap.

This time our cab took us both home, and somehow, they seemed to enjoy what had just happened. As it turns out, they had only gone a block or so away, figuring we would be needing a cab again, in a very short time. They were right!

BUM BUM CONTEST AT THE ZOO

With winter in Inuvik being extremely long and cold, and with limited sun, you need to find ways to keep yourself busy. We managed to do that with what we perceived as fun things. You know, the kind of things that you and your friends can tell stories about for years after, as I am attempting now! You just can't make this fun up! Oh, the stupid shit we did.

A lot of our fun happened at the Mackenzie Hotel. Walter let our group of friends have the run of the bar. Like a mentioned in a previous story, Brian P, Guy, and me started a company called Damad Productions and Consulting that we operated in the Mackenzie Hotel to help bring in patrons for Walter. Did everything we try work out perfectly? The short answer is no. Did people still have fun? Yes! Did anybody get hurt during our fun? The short answer is yes. Did we know exactly what we were doing? No, but we would carry on as if we knew how everything was going to go. We thought we were professionals, that was our goal. As it turned out, "shit happens".

We tossed around a bunch of ideas for Saturday events to fill the bar. This is the one and only, and I mean the only, time this was ever done. We never tried it again…never! We planned the Famous Bum Bum Contest in hopes of a full house. We advertised on the radio, put posters up everywhere, and word of mouth also worked well for most anything in this small community. The three of us worked hard to get this contest just right. We wanted nothing short of perfection. We were "professionals" after all.

In order to do this contest, we needed some props. Brian P. was in charge of the prop department. He needed to make a big wooden wall with six large round holes equally spaced that would stand on its own. The audience was going to be on one side while our participants were going to be hidden on the other side. My job was to be the MC for the evening. Guy sold tickets at the front door, so that people could come watch the performance. With us being "professionals", we had everything covered and nothing could possibly go wrong!

Setting this all up took time. We wanted it to be perfect, but I think it was because we were drinking a lot while getting stuff ready for all the fun. We placed that big wall right in the middle of the dance floor. We didn't use up any space where the crowd would be sitting, and we needed some space on the other side of that wall.

People started to come in and actually paying us the two dollar fee to watch, and hopefully buy lots of drinks, which was the main purpose of this event. Of course, we dragged our feet getting set up so that would happen. We wanted the booze to loosen up the crowd as we were going to need them a bit drunk for this.

161

The bar was literally at full capacity, which surprised all of us, even Walter. He was happy to see his place so full. It was loud with people in various stages of pure drunkenness. It was getting crazy in there, but we stalled some more. The band played one set while people drank. Everyone was wondering what that thing with the six holes was all about, but we didn't let any secrets out. We needed six volunteers from the crowd, and they didn't need to know why until it was show time!

We were satisfied with how everything looked. The crowd was noisy and laughter filled the air. It was my turn to get to work. It was much like being at a sporting event, a loud sporting event...not like a chess game at all! It took a bit of time, but I managed to get everybody quiet enough so that I could talk to the audience. First, I asked for six volunteers from the crowd, who would be willing participants. "Could you just please raise your hands, if you're interested." Damn, a lot of hands went up, considering they had no idea what was going to happen...but in their defence, neither did we!

With all three of us standing in front of the crowd, we had to pick a few popular people who were known in the bar. People that people knew is what we were after. We got that done and now we had our six contestants. Five guys and one girl were picked. We asked them stand up in front of the wall for a minute so the entire bar would know who they were. Then, Brian P. ushered them behind the great wall full of holes.

The place was loud. There was lots of noise, more yelling, just what a bar sounds like when it's full of mostly happy people waiting for something fun to happen. After all, this was new to all of them, as well as us! "Time to get this party started!" I yell out. Above the noise, I had to explain what we had planned... it's go time! I get the crowd somewhat settled down, and asked if they could give me a "Hell Ya" when I named each of the six,

162

if they knew that person. I was quite shocked to hear some very loud Hell Ya's for each participant that would be behind the wall. Perfect. We needed these folks to be well known in town.

Again, I had to settle the crowd a bit so that I could explain the contest. First, I say that in a few minutes, the holes in that wall will have naked bums sticking through them. That made everyone start up loud again, but I was expecting something like that. I just let them settle down, then went on to explain that Guy was going to have them vote with a "Hell Ya" on the bum that matched the name. The loudest votes would have the name posted above the bum, then we would continue to the next butt. The crowd's job was to help us by their loud whistling and yelling to decide whose bum was whose bum.

Guy was beside the first bum. He was to use a black marker and in big letters write the name of the guy above the bum that got the most noise. Easy. The hard part was setting everything up. Hours and hours we had put in to have this bar filled. I explained that once all the names were on the board, we would bring all six out fully clothed to stand beside the hole where they had stuck their bums in for all to see. Again, this was going to be easy. How the hell anything can go wrong with this simple contest in a room full of drunk people, being very loud, is beyond me, but...

Being "professionals", we never liked the word "but" at the end of a sentence.

Everything was going great for us. The bar was full to standing room only and people were having loud fun instead of fighting. Walter was making money. We got the money from the entrance of the bar, plus free drinks. But, right after all six bums showed up in those holes, with Guy standing beside the very first one, the guys and girl behind the wall started trying to wiggle their bums in the holes to garner attention from the crowd. I think we had told them they would win a prize or something to that effect, if the crowd would guess right. Now, the real "but".

These guys were wiggling and jiggling so much that the entire wall fell completely on the floor. The crowd really started laughing and yelling as the six were still bent over wiggling and squirming their asses. With all the noise and excitement going on, they didn't notice that the crowd could see all of them, as Brian P.'s prop laid on the floor. We didn't even get past the very first contestant when shit went sideways, and the crowd loved it.

I had my face covered in my hands as I couldn't stop laughing. It did take a minute or two before one of the guys noticed everyone could see them all bent over at the waist, bums out front and centre.

Yep, even "professionals" can have a bad day when dealing with the unknown.

I TAKE A BEATING IN
MY OWN HOME

During the rather long and cold winters in Inuvik, our homes, built sitting high up on pilings (telephone poles would be a more accurate description), would snap, crackle, and pop as the permafrost would move the building. These sounds, during -45° to -50° weather, sounded like gunshots out of a high powered rifle, and most times would make you jump straight up in bed wondering what the hell just happened!

Leading into every single building were utilidors. They were totally insulated culverts to protect the water and sewer lines. These were like mazes all over town connecting every building. Plumbing could not be put in the ground as the permafrost would make servicing any of this impossible. These utilidors around town all had separate heights, depending on how high the building was perched and the slope of the area. They had steps going up and over wherever it made sense. They were too high to climb over and yet too low to slide under if you were carrying anything. Some roadways were built under them, so at times you drove right under the plumbing utilidors. They also made a great path way if you walked on the very top of them. You could go from one end of town to the other if you got on the right one. If someone was walking on it while it was really cold out, that walking sound on cold tin and snow sounded loud…almost like somebody was right inside your house!

Winters also made our place twist and turn in the cold…the doors would not work right. As a matter of fact, our bedroom door wouldn't close. In fact, it never closed at all during the winters. I found that I could hang my house coat up on the door, which would prevent someone from looking in. Not the best security, but hey, it was a housecoat. How tough could it be?

Brian P., Lois and I had been out to the bar for the night, and when we came home, we found a snowdrift in our kitchen. This happened when the wind was just right, as that door didn't shut tight either. Sometimes living in Inuvik, you kept a shovel inside your house and one outside your house to get you in or out!

We had our normal nightcaps after coming home, then off to bed we went as tomorrow was another day. Brian P. went to his room, Lois and I to ours, but not before stuffing a winter coat under the big gap in the kitchen door to keep the snow out.

Once in our bedroom, I hung my housecoat on the top of the door to cover the big gap that was there all winter. The colder it got, the bigger the gap became!

We were both sound asleep when I awoke suddenly to the sounds of footsteps right in our hallway. I couldn't believe it; we had an intruder inside, which really was not all that uncommon in Inuvik. When I got the sleep out of my eyes, I could just make out the outline of the guy standing right in our bedroom doorway. He was just standing there watching us, as the walking noise had stopped. In the darkness it was impossible to see his face. I slowly and quietly whispered for Lois to wake up, "There is somebody watching us from the door." Once I had her awake, she confirmed there was somebody there…again I whispered to her, "I am going to jump up and rush this guy. As soon as I do, turn the lights on and call police." Lois pointed out that I was naked, but I wasn't going to let being naked get in the way of a good fight, not in our home!

It was now or never. I made my move and jumped from the bed and ran head on to grab this stranger. He never moved a bit as I jumped at him. The lights came on and with Lois on the phone to the police, I hit my damn head so hard on the door it knocked me backwards with my house coat in my arms and on top of me. This guy in the door was my own housecoat!

Right about then Lois was gasping for air, as she was laughing so hard at what she just witnessed from her front row seat. "How tough can a housecoat be?" Well, my housecoat was tough enough to leave a big red welt on my forehead, from hitting the housecoat and then the door.

I'm not sure how, but everyone in the Legion heard about this little fight that I lost against my housecoat by the very next day. I couldn't even say the old saying, "You should see the other guy"!

A SHOT IN THE DARK

My good friend Glenn, better known as Piggy to all his friends, was a man with many friends in town, and most communities surrounding our world up north. He was a very well-liked man who would go way out of his way to help most anybody, at any time of the day or night. He was a good man, and I'm proud to have been one of his good friends back in the day.

Piggy and I had been talking about going moose hunting on one of the nice days that winter would surprise us with. All you needed to go hunting was a nice day, a hunting licence, a gun, of course, some survival gear, bullets, and each man needed a snowmobile. I had all those things except the snowmobile.

Luckily, my friend Guy had a machine to lend me, but it wasn't meant for pulling heavy things. As a matter of fact, it was built for speed, and man that thing was fast! Piggy had a great machine for hunting in the deep snow, one that could pull and was meant for exactly what we were going to put it through on the day of our hunt.

We finally were supposed to get a nice weekend and decided that Saturday was going to be our day of hunting. Piggy was hunting for his rather big family to feed, while I was hunting for Lois and me. We had full intention of bringing back at least three moose that day, which would last a long time for the both of us.

Finding moose is not all that easy. Like when you are away from town, you can see for a very long ways across the tundra. That means so can the moose. There were also patches of shrubs that those big buggers could hide in, so you needed to always be aware of all your surroundings. Being aware was something you always did when you left the security of town, even if you just were going for a drive with the truck. You needed to know how quick the weather can turn on you. The north is nice, but it can be brutal at the same time.

As the weather guy promised, Saturday started out as a very good day for two guys to get out of town and look for moose meat for the family. It was only -20the morning when we started out. Once we were away from town, we picked a spot way off in the distance, and worked our way towards that, in hopes of just seeing some meat. We had travelled across frozen lakes, around thick willows, across open country. We even stopped at one point and sat on our machines while we had a smoke and some food...hell, -20°C was a perfect day, so far!

This time of year, we hardly had any sun. We knew that once it went down for the day it was hard to see very far past your headlight on the snowmobile. Some say it gets as dark as the inside of a cow's belly when you are out on the land this time of year...and I believe that to be true.

The day had been perfect for hunting... well not so much at this point. We drove some more and kept looking at those shrubs in hopes of finding even just one moose, since it was starting to get a bit late on us. We also both noticed that the temperature was dropping faster than we had expected, too. We carried on though, and as most hunters will tell you, you always go a bit further than you've intended, as you think something will show up just over the next rise or in the shrubs. I guess I'm saying that we still had hope on our side.

With hope on our minds, we carried on with the idea we would just get to high ground. That way we could use the binoculars to have one good last look around before heading back to town. It was getting cold now and not much light was left. We needed to hurry things up and start heading back, while our tracks were still visible in the headlights.

Like I've said before, things can change in a hurry in the north. There, standing right in front of us, were the moose we were looking for. Excitement was the right word for this moment. Both of us were trying to get our rifles loaded and get to shooting. My gun had gotten so cold that the firing pin would not work. Piggy's rifle also did not fire. It was damn cold, but no time to worry about that yet. We both used our cigarette lighters to warm up the bolts on the guns, while the moose just stood there, as if they didn't care that we were within spitting distance of them.

We had all those groceries standing right there, as we frantically ran the lighters up and down the cold steel of our guns, in hopes to get at least one working. It felt like forever until the guns were warm enough to fire. We took aim and we managed to get three, even after all that shit was going on trying to get one gun to work!

Now that we had our moose laying in the snow, we noticed our second change: the weather was way worse. The wind was picking up and it started snowing hard. We were going to be in trouble if we didn't hurry and get these back to town, which was about 30 miles away… but in what direction? We had tied one of the moose to my borrowed sled and tied the remaining two moose to Piggy's sled. His machine was much better for pulling than my speed machine, which proved almost useless right now.

We only went a little way when Piggy stopped and just sat on his machine looking around. It was fucking cold out now. I rode up and asked him what was wrong. He looked at me and said, "I don't have any idea which way to go". Okay, if I ever told anybody that I've never been scared, I lied. Piggy knew his way around the tundra as good as anybody, but with the wind having picked up, we couldn't see a damn thing. Even our original tracks were snow covered and it was way past dark.

I was officially scared for the both of us. Another rule in the north is never go look for anybody in a storm of any kind, and if it's dark, wait until morning to go look. We both knew that, and didn't expect any help coming from Inuvik at all. After some discussion we decided on a plan. It was slightly better than just flipping a coin for the direction.

Trying to drag a moose through the deep snow proved to be way too much to ask of my borrowed machine. It quit on us, and we just left it with the moose still tied on behind it. I jumped on Piggy's snowmobile behind him. Luckily for me, my friend was a big, strong fellow, the kind of guy you need in a time like this.

My good friend, Glenn (Piggy)

He blocked the wind for me as I stayed low behind him. We slowly made our way through the darkness to who knows where.

It's hard to describe just how bitter cold it was with the wind howling all around us. We had to yell just to talk to each other, and we were on the same machine. We crept along determined to get home.

We got stuck several times and had to both pull the moose by hand to get enough slack in the rope to move the sled. Night was upon us, we were short of fuel, and we weren't getting far. Suddenly, we were heading down hill fast. Way too fast! We couldn't see the terrain change through the darkness. We hit the bottom hard and Piggy turned his sled to the left which broke loose the two moose. They ended up coming to a stop in a big patch of willows. There was no chance that we could get them untangled in that mess with it being so brutally cold, windy, and dark.

I must say that in all my years in the north, I had never found myself in such a situation. The three things that would normally keep you in town were cold, wind and dark, and yet, we were somewhere out in all that shit. Even though we were both very scared for our lives, we didn't show it. We calmly just drove away from those two moose. Now, it was just the two of us on the one snowmobile.

I never second-guessed Piggy's direction, as he drove us through that brutal night, in the hope of seeing some light somewhere. With the swirling and blowing snow all around us it was what you would call just a "shot in the dark" or a "hope for the best". Our trail was filling in behind us in a matter of seconds, not minutes. We couldn't even tell if we had drove here already. We had decided that we would just continue to drive till we either got to town, ran out of gas or broke down. If it was the latter, we would just dig ourselves into the snow and wait until morning. We knew people would come looking for us in the morning for sure…but getting through a night like this with limited supplies, may be a big problem. Luckily, we smoked and both had lighters, so getting a fire started would be possible.

We had left Inuvik at about 10:00 am. It was now around midnight, and we were running low on gas, hope, and strength. Both of us were shivering, and we knew what that meant.

Things were getting bleak for us both and we knew it. But like I said earlier, things can change in an instant in the north, and this was one of those times. The wind calmed down a bit which stopped most of the swirling snow, and then we saw the glimmer of the town lights far off in the darkness. It was not bright, but we could both see the faint lights of Inuvik!

It was 2:00 am when we finally got to town. I went straight to bed and tried to warm my body up. It was not working. Lois said I felt like an ice cube. It was for good reason; it was -35°C out. I stayed in bed all the next day, still shivering on and off, while Piggy was doing the same at his house. He asked some of his family to go look for our three moose and one snowmobile. I believe a fellow from town took his airplane up before they headed out to look, and he spotted our left behind items. He relayed the information to the guys that were going to retrieve them, and everything was brought back, while neither Piggy nor I could even get out of bed.

To this very day, even as I write this story, I can still feel a chill run up my back. I have talked with Piggy and he feels the same. We should have died that night; really, we should have died. One good reason we didn't die was because of my hunting partner, Glenn. Without him, I would not have made it back to town at all. The other reason we didn't die was because of my mother. She worked in a Catholic church for many years and she is the closet person to God that I know. I believe she was my guardian angel. Those are the two reasons why I'm writing this book today.

Thank you, Piggy. Your "shot in the dark" was a perfect shot; and thank you, Mom for your guidance that night, as you helped Piggy steer us in the right direction.

GUY AND THE FLUX

I felt lucky to be working at one of the industrial supply stores in Inuvik with the best crew of weird people. There was never a dull moment. Some moments were down right hilarious, at least for some of us! With practical jokes being an almost daily occurrence, we all would be on high alert. Each and every one of us could only hope that we were not the one being targeted, as we were targeting one of the others. Some days you could be so entrenched in your own ideas of who you were trying to get one over on, you wouldn't notice the attack coming your way. Staying alert to your surroundings was paramount!

Then there were the fun things that just happened all on their own. No practical joke can override the importance of something very funny that happens to another while you watch and just let things play out on their own. This is one of those stories.

There was no set up beforehand, this all happened via karma, I suppose. I had a front row seat to what was one of the funniest moments... so funny, we still talk about it today.

Myrna was a tiny, quiet talking, very polite and shy lady who did stained glass work in Inuvik. She was just plain awesome all the way around. Her tiny body had a ton of talent when it came to this art she loved. To do stained glass you need flux. This item is usually used for soldering tiny wires, so that they don't come loose. Myrna used it for other things, better things. She made awesome stained glass with the help of the flux.

I'm not sure why, but Myrna never came into our building. Maybe it was because we were a few miles out of town; maybe she was too nervous; or maybe she didn't like to drive out her way. She would always phone Guy, the boss of all us crazies, to place her order and then wait for our freight truck. It usually came every two weeks bringing 20-25 pallets of freight. The normal routine was for Myrna to talk with Guy, and only Guy. Somehow she felt comfy with him, and that's who she would deal with on her flux orders.

Our freight trucks were almost never on time. The roads in winter can stop freight from getting to town, which was another annoyance that we all had to live with in the far north.

Today, we didn't need any practical jokes. Today, we didn't need to try anything on anybody. Today was going to work out just funny all on its own.

Today was the perfect storm, and was heading straight towards Guy. What's even better, is that none of us could see it coming.

Our front counter had a phone on it. Every desk had a phone, and if you were a customer standing in front of the counter, you would see a row of parts books on top of tall filing cabinets along the wall on our side…the office side!

Here's where it gets interesting for all of us… well, almost all of us. Guy had come out of his office in a big rush; that's how he worked, always busy and always fast-paced. Well, that was good as far as the job went, but it also made him a target in many practical jokes, as his guard was down when he was busy.

Guy headed straight to the parts book against the wall to get some information for the order he was working on, which put his back to the front counter. I was sitting at my desk, and Wayne was sitting at his, which was pointed to the front counter. From his desk he could see all the customers that came into the building. My desk had me sitting sideways, but I could see the customers at the front counter from my chair as well.

So, Wayne is at his desk, I'm at mine, and Guy has his back turned to the counter, oblivious to everything else going on, as he's thinking about what he is doing. He's lost in his own thoughts.

I hear the front door open. I wait a bit and then I see Myrna quietly standing at the front counter. Now, I was kind of lazy, so I looked over at Wayne to see if he was going to go look after Myrna, but shit! Just then, the damn phone started to ring. Wayne grabbed that call, so I headed over to see what Myrna needed, knowing full well that Guy was too busy to help her today.

I asked what I could help her with, and she answered me in her little mouse-like shy voice, "Do you know if my flux has come in yet?" As I pointed out, I was kind of lazy, so instead of going to check in the freight for customer orders, I just turned around and asked the one person who usually looked after her with these words, "Hey Guy, do you know if Myrna's flux has come in yet?"

Now shit gets crazy for a few minutes here...

Guy wildly throws his hands into the air and without even turning around, he starts this insane, long, loud monologue about the flux in question.

"NO THE FLUX IS NOT HERE! I TOLD HER I WOULD LET HER KNOW WHEN IT FLUXING CAME IN. WHY THE FLUX IS SHE CALLING NOW? TELL HER I DON'T KNOW WHEN THE FLUXING STUFF WILL ARRIVE. TELL HER TO FLUX OFF AND JUST FLUXING WAIT FOR MY CALL, FOR FLUX SAKES!"... all the while I'm standing right across the counter from Myrna and I can't even do anything to stop Guy. He was on a roll!

He was just slowing down his verbal diarrhea when I quietly said, as I looked her straight in the eye, "Sounds like your flux is not in yet, Myrna," to which she quietly responded, "That's okay, Randy. I'll wait for Guy's FLUXING call."

It was right then that Guy turned around, and for a brief moment he stared right at Myrna and myself, then he took off at a very fast pace all the way to his office at the other end of the trailer, to go hide I suppose. Wayne also got to witness the entire event right from the comfort of his old chair at his desk. Myrna walked out of the door, and as soon as she was out of the building, Wayne and I couldn't control the laughter.

It was the perfect storm. Guy had heard the phone ring. It only rang twice and quit, then a moment later, I was asking about the flux. In Guy's defence, he thought Myrna was on the phone, and that it had been me who picked up the call. I just happened to be lucky enough to see it all with Myrna standing right beside me...ah, the joy of watching a friend go down in flames all on his own.

ACKNOWLEDGMENTS

Without my Uncle Dick and Aunt Lucille living in Inuvik at a time when I was looking for a place to be, this book wouldn't be in your hands. They saved me from all my troubles in Brandon, Manitoba, and gave me a fighting chance in this world.

Terry Babiy called me at home one day and asked me to come into town for coffee and a chat. We had a long coffee talk about my health and what was keeping me busy, and my dilemma about struggling to write my stories. He told me, "Just write one book and give it to your son." I felt like I finally had a plan. As we were leaving, he said he had the perfect name for my book. Call it "Day to Day". Thank you, my friend. Terry knows all we chatted about that day, but this was what I needed the most. Without Terry, this book wouldn't be in your hands.

Teena Toker, my very good friend, also helped me. I was in the infant stages of trying to write this book. We had gotten together to have a little party fun night at our house. During the night, we started talking about my book. Teena says, "You should add in the name of the book 'The Blurry Years'"... So, a big thank you to Teena for helping name the book.

A big thank you to Kirk (Scruff) Stephen, my friend and first mate on my boat any time he could come with me. With him in the boat I felt much safer. He always sat right up beside me watching the river for marker buoys, sticks in the mud, and mixed my drinks for me. Without his help in navigating the Mackenzie River during the scariest of storms, this book wouldn't be in your hands. Thank you, Buddy, for keeping us safe!

My wife Lois knows everything that is in this book. She helped me with editing, and reminding me of the way some stories went. Lois supports me with every step I take. She has also kept me alive enough to get this first book out. There were many scary moments for us during the years it has taken me to write these stories. Without Lois in my corner, this book wouldn't be in your hands. Thank you so much, Lois…I love you!

I also want to thank important family and friends in the book who have passed on before they could read about it themselves:

Uncle Dick…RIP Dec 5, 2013. I miss you!

Aunt Lucille… RIP June 23, 2012. I miss you!

Charles (Charlie) Ryan… RIP Nov 11, 2022. I miss you!

Guy Willy… RIP Sept 1, 2023. I miss you!

ABOUT THE AUTHOR

The stories you will read in this book will tell all you need to know about the author. But what they won't tell you is this:

Randy Day was born in 1957 in Killarney, Manitoba, a little town in southern Manitoba. From there, the family moved to Dunrea, Manitoba, another small town about a 30-minute drive north of Killarney. After a few years of living there, his dad got a job in Brandon, Manitoba, where they remained for many years. Randy attended Earl Oxford, Earl Haig, and Neelin High School while in Brandon. He loved doing all the sports he could in school, but getting him to stay in the important classes was tough!

Somewhere along the way, he inherited the nickname "Zip". His older brother, Darryl, had a nickname of "Do Dah", so it's plain to see that "Zippity Do Dah Day" was a natural.

In 1976, Randy and his girlfriend went to Inuvik. Randy's Uncle Dick needed a sheet metal apprentice and had offered it to him, and that's why he went way up north. Back in 1976, going that far seemed like the end of the world. Randy and girlfriend flew back to Brandon to get married, and flew right back to Inuvik. That marriage didn't work out, and he went back to Brandon, and got a divorce.

Randy moved back to Inuvik in the early 1980s after the Brandon City Police advised him to return and "not come back for 7 years". Once back in Inuvik, things felt so much better to Randy. He ended up getting his journeyman ticket for industrial warehousing, which led him into management jobs a few years down the road.

Randy met his second wife, Lois, in Inuvik and now, 36 years later, they are still married with one son named Scotty.

In retirement (forced by cancer), Randy started writing these stories. He took some time to do live theatre and a few TV commercials, then completed this book.

Manufactured by Amazon.ca
Acheson, AB

13321863R00107